JOE BIDEN'S
DELAWARE

JOE BIDEN'S
DELAWARE

DAN SHORTRIDGE

THE
History
PRESS

Published by The History Press
Charleston, SC
www.historypress.com

First published 2024

Manufactured in the United States

ISBN 9781467157698

Library of Congress Control Number: 2024938217

This book is dedicated to the life and memory of Steve Norton.
He is missed so much.

CONTENTS

ACKNOWLEDGEMENTS AND THANKS

As a former journalist, I see history as a longer form of reporting: sifting through tales, facts, dates and narratives to tell a coherent story. Sometimes, it sheds light; other times, it explores new topics at length.

This book would not be possible without the work of so many other reporters who came before. Their contributions were invaluable, tracing the trail of Joe Biden's life through episodes long since forgotten.

The reporters of all stripes—local, regional, and national—on whose work I relied, deserve an incredible amount of gratitude. Please thank a reporter when you next meet one. My personal thanks go out to Kayla Adler, Travis M. Andrews, Emily Barrett, Cris Barrish, Paul Bedard, Kate Bennett, Robin Brown, Scott Cameron, Al Cartwright, Randall Chase, Celia Cohen, Ellen Driscoll, Mark Eichmann, Margie Fishman, Chris Flood, Dennis Forney, Bill Frank, Bob Frump, Richard Gaw, Pam George, Katie Glueck, Carl Hamilton, Jane Harriman, Suzanne Herel, Jason Hoffman, Christina Jedra, Tamara Keith, Kitty Kelley, Edward L. Kenney, Paul Kiefer, Rachel Kipp, Rachel Kurzius, Mike Lang, Ann Marie Linnabery, Norman Lockman, Christopher Maag, Ron MacArthur, Ken Mammarella, Marilyn Mather, Ryan Mavity, Jessica McDowell, Maureen Milford, Beth Miller, Zeke Miller, Jeff Mordock, Ralph Moyed, Jeff Neiburg, Meredith Newman, Jack Nolan, Amie Parnes, Josephine Peterson, Antonio Prado, Jarek Rutz, Kevin Shalvey, Robert Shogan, Bill Shull, Barbara Sprunt, Jonathan Starkey, Darlene Superville, Katie Tabeling, Patricia Talorico, Casey Tolan, Alex Vuocolo, Tom Warwick, Abby Weiss, Will Weissert, Ron Williams, Xerxes Wilson,

Cathy Wolff and Terry Zintl. Included here as well are the numerous anonymous and uncredited reporters and news assistants who wrote articles in the days before bylines.

The photographs in this book come from a variety of sources. Special thanks are due to Mary Allen of Widener University; D.J. McAneny of the Office of U.S. Senator Chris Coons; and the staff of the Delaware Public Archives, who, as always, do an amazingly thorough job and go out of their way to make a researcher feel at home. Some photographs are courtesy of the Barack Obama Presidential Library; the Chairman of the Joint Chiefs of Staff; the Delaware Public Archives; the Delaware State Senate; the Library of Congress; the National Guard Bureau; the Office of Governor Jack Markell; the Office of U.S. Senator Chris Coons; Rachel Kipp; the U.S. Air Force; the U.S. Air National Guard; the U.S. Army; the U.S. Navy; *The Whale*; the White House; and Widener University.

All that said, any errors that have crept in, including any names that may be absent from the previous lists, are my mistakes and solely my responsibility.

Special thanks are owed to Kate Jenkins, my liaison with The History Press, who kept me on task and ahead of my deadlines.

I especially need to express gratitude to my wife, Rachel Kipp, who is always my best editor, adviser, motivator and inspiration. Our kids, Dassi, Matty and Liam, are an immense source of joy and make me proud every day.

PREFACE

When I die, Delaware will be written on my heart.
—Joe Biden[1]

Joe Biden goes by just one name in Delaware. He's the Madonna or Cher of this tiny state. You say three letters, and people instantly know who you mean. By the end of his run in the Senate, his campaign bumper stickers just said: "JOE."[2]

This book is about Joe, his family, the people who loved them and the places that shaped Joe's career and rise to the White House. It's important to understand that Delaware works by the power of people. We're a small enough state that relationships really matter; if you say something disparaging about a person, chances are decent that you may be talking to their cousin or an in-law. At the same time, the population has changed dramatically over the last two decades as more retirees from New York, New Jersey and Pennsylvania have entered seeking low taxes and a coastal environment.

For most of modern history, the state's economy has been dominated by chemicals (DuPont, Hercules), chickens (Perdue, Mountaire, Allen's) and credit cards (MBNA).[3] Today, chickens remain the only dominant industry of those three Cs; the business-friendly Chancery court has joined them as a driving economic force.

Just about everyone in Delaware has a Joe story. Mine took place in high school, when I participated in a YMCA Youth in Government program and attended a conference in Washington, D.C., in the hot, muggy summer of

1997. We ate lunch on Capitol Hill and invited our home state members of Congress to stop in and speak for a few minutes, as their busy schedules permitted. Joe arrived with just a few minutes left before the end of the lunch. He flashed his infectious grin and spoke for a full—and inspiring—forty-five minutes. He was the only member of Congress at that event to receive a standing ovation from some pretty cynical, hard-boiled, teenaged future politicians. They were all abuzz with Joe-mania, conservatives and liberals alike praising his performance.

What we had all felt was the "Biden Rush," as Richard Ben Cramer had described years earlier:

> *Joe would get to talking fast, with conviction—something near joy in his voice—and he'd haul them along, until they could feel his belief like a hand on their backs, until they could see it as he could, until the thing was shining in the air…and they only hoped they were good enough to be with him, there, at the end.…You could feel the thing happen in the room—the "connect."*[4]

My daughter's story is about Joe's late son, Beau, who served as Delaware's attorney general for two terms. When my daughter was younger, we visited my parents in Laurel for the Fourth of July festivities. Beau was walking in the town's parade on the opposite side of Central Avenue from where we stood. As soon as he saw my daughter waving from the sidewalk, he did a quick left turn and veered directly over. He knelt in front of her and chatted for a good two to three minutes, completely ignoring the voting-age parents and grandparents surrounding her. I was impressed. She was entranced—and saddened when, years later, Beau was felled by cancer.

Recognizing the dynamic of Joe and the Bidens is as much about understanding Delaware as it is about understanding a president and a family. Delaware is a small state—tiny, even. As Hunter Biden says, it is "easy to miss on a map if you're not looking for it."[5] For decades, Delaware politics was dominated by two names: Bayard and DuPont. The two families seemed to trade off offices and vie for control. "The Delaware story reads in large part like a Morse code: Bayard, Bayard, Dupont; Bayard, DuPont, Bayard; DuPont, DuPont, Bayard," wrote Professor Ezra Bowen of Pennsylvania's Lafayette College in 1925. "If you live in this smallest state and you have no Bayard or DuPont connection of blood, business, or politics, you are a farmer or a shopkeeper, a purveyor to the host."[6]

Joe Biden was no shopkeeper or farmer—and certainly no purveyor. He burst onto the scene under his own power, unseating the old guard and

The official presidential portrait of Joe Biden, taken at the White House in the library room. Biden ran for president three times, finally succeeding in 2020. *Library of Congress.*

launching the start of a new era in Delaware politics. As Celia Cohen, the retired dean of the Delaware journalist corps, notes: "Delaware has yielded only one Joe Biden."[7]

As exemplified by Biden's thirty-six years in the Senate, Delaware's political leaders are noted for their longevity. "We don't have elections. We have coronations," remarked one former state Democratic chairman.

One particularly notable foursome dominated the state's politics for a decade and a half: Joe Biden and Bill Roth in the U.S. Senate, Mike Castle in the governor's mansion and Congress and Tom Carper in Congress and the governor's mansion. Except for Castle and Carper's "swap" in 1992, the lineup did not change. In Cohen's words, they were a "veritable Mount Rushmore, half-Democrat and half-Republican in testament to the institutionalized bipartisanship here."[8] Some of that overt bipartisanship has faded away in recent years, as the Republican Party has lost relevance and power in Delaware, but the trappings remain.

In recent years, the "Delaware Way" has come under fire and criticism, especially from the rising progressive tide in the First State. "Its defenders argue that in a state that small…politics naturally hinges on consensus, long-term relationships, and bipartisan bonhomie," writes *Politico* reporter Ben Schreckinger. "Its detractors see a backwater wracked with cronyism."

Joe Biden does not count himself as a detractor of Delaware's famed way. "We need a little more of the Delaware Way," he said before entering the 2020 election. "We've got to make it more the American way, and it's lost. Our politics has become so mean, so petty, so vicious that we can't

Delaware's solid foursome in 1996 (*left to right*): Representative Mike Castle, Governor Tom Carper, Senator Bill Roth and Senator Joe Biden. *Delaware Public Archives.*

The year after Beau's death, Joe Biden attended the Veterans' Day event at the Delaware Memorial Bridge in 2016. To the left is Governor Jack Markell. *U.S. Army National Guard.*

govern ourselves, in many cases, even talk to one another. It can't go on like this, folks."[9]

Above all, for many years, civility controlled the state's political scene. Few candidates got down into the gutter; those who did were quickly cashiered out. As Beau Biden described it: "Even when my dad's been hit the hardest at any point over thirty-six years, he's rarely if ever engaged in the cheap shot that is the give-and-take of politics. That's just not what he is, and never has been."[10]

This book pays tribute to a bygone era. The economy, the politics, the governing—all have changed irrevocably. Delaware is different now than it was years ago. Many of the places where the Biden family worked, ate and played during Joe's childhood, early career and Senate years are gone. But by recalling them—and how they shaped Joe and Delaware in ways both small and large—today, we can conjure and capture memories that are both poignant and powerful.

This book is not a strict biography but a chronicle of people, places and institutions against a backdrop of a person's life. Most readers already know the basic outline of Biden's story: his Senate career, his family, his tragedies, his campaigns for the White House. Some items are placed out of chronological order to allow for a smoother story. This does not pretend to be a comprehensive chronology, but it is, I hope, a useful and personal addition to the body of work about one of the most important presidents of our time.

Through the pages that follow, you will come across references to people by both their first and last names, such as Joe and Jill. I mean no disrespect to anyone; that usage is simply to avoid excessive repetition of the last name Biden and to distinguish one Biden from another.

Joe Biden's life has been shaped by Delaware—and our lives by his. Whatever his future holds, I hope that you enjoy this book and the history it brings forward.

—Dan Shortridge

1

THE EARLY YEARS

Joe Biden is a proud son of Scranton, Pennsylvania. His family roots run deep there. But the roots he set for himself are firmly placed in Delaware.

His family moved to the state in pursuit of a job in 1953, the year Joe turned eleven.[11] His father, Joe Sr., had lived in Wilmington before he married Joe's mom, Jean. The Bidens had a traditional household, with Joe working many different jobs as the primary breadwinner. During tough times in Scranton, Joe Sr. got a job as a boiler cleaner for a heating, ventilation and air conditioning company in Delaware, driving back and forth across the 140-mile stretch, a long and draining commute.[12]

Eventually, the family packed up and moved to Delaware. They chose the Claymont area at the northern tip of the state, close to the Pennsylvania border. Brookview Apartments was located off Philadelphia Pike; the new two-story home was white with columns out front. Across the road stood a former mansion known as Archmere, now a school, which drew Joe like a magnet and would eventually play a role in his children's lives.[13]

Joe started in the third grade in Delaware—he was actually a repeat because he had missed a lot of that school year in Scranton after his tonsils and adenoids had been removed. His school was Holy Rosary in Claymont, along Philadelphia Pike.[14] The school at Holy Rosary, founded around 1950, was built and supported by the greatest generation, those who had served in World War II and created thriving communities in the postwar era "so that we might be who we are today," Bishop William Koenig remarked at the parish's one hundredth anniversary celebration in 2022. (The event was attended by parishioner Anne Carney and her son Governor John Carney, who also attended Holy Rosary School.)[15] The school was originally built with eight classrooms to hold 150 students in order to accommodate the growing parish population: "At the present time it is of vital importance to care for the many elementary grade children who have come into the Claymont parish in the past few years," children such as the Bidens, a reporter noted.[16]

The nuns at Holy Rosary instructed students in the scholastic arts of history, math, geography, reading and writing. The Catholic doctrine also brought with it instruction in the fundamental principles of "decency, fair play, and virtue," Joe later recalled. "You didn't give your life, but it was noble to help a lady across a street. It was noble to offer a hand up to somebody who had less. It was noble to step in when the bully was picking on somebody. It was noble to intervene."[17]

Those moral lessons were ingrained in the children's heads. At Holy Rosary, Joe once took the blame for another student's eraser toss. He stayed after school in detention. "When you intervene, you have to stand up and take the consequences," Joe later remembered. But the students had an affection for their teacher-disciplinarians, piling the nuns' desks high with soaps as Christmas gifts.[18]

Biden was also cognizant of his important role as a big brother to his sister, Valerie. She tagged along with him, and he stood up for her, including her in everything. "Wherever he went I was there and the guys just accepted me," she recalled. "He was a wonderful, wonderful brother, and what he did through all my years growing up was, he always watched out for me, but he never acted like he was doing me a favor. On the other hand, I always watched out for him."[19]

Two years later, in 1955, the Bidens bought a new home in the community of Mayfield. They were the fourth family to move into the brand-new development, devoid of trees and shade. Joe Sr. was a bit of an anomaly in the neighborhood, which was mostly populated by young professionals—chemists, accountants and lawyers—who primarily worked at DuPont, then a driving economic powerhouse. For those workers, DuPont in Delaware was a symbol of job security, and Mayfield was a "way station for these young men working their way up the corporate ladder," Joe wrote.[20] For the Bidens, Mayfield was also a temporary stopping point, but it was a move up from the apartment complex.[21]

The Bidens had to drive farther to attend Sunday mass, as Mayfield was mostly Protestant, and Joe transferred to St. Helena's, just a few blocks away.[22] It was there that Biden was ridiculed by a nun for his stuttering, and it was there that Jean Finnegan Biden showed her son what advocacy meant—and the important role of being a parent. Uncowed by the nuns' habits and position in her church, Jean spoke with fire to defend her son. "If you every speak to my son like that again, I'll come back and rip that bonnet off your head. Do you understand me?" she told the nun.[23]

Holy Rosary and Saint Helena's both continued until 2008, when they merged into a single school with just over 280 students in grades pre-K through eight. Declining student populations forced the diocese's hand, but leaders were determined to preserve the best parts of the schools' identities and create new traditions. The new school was named Pope John Paul II, honoring one of the longest-serving pontiffs in Roman Catholic history.[24] "The decline came as part of an entire shift in how people saw education for their children. People are now consumers of an educational product, with a more vested interest in how that school should work, where as a generation or two ago, you simply just went to your neighborhood for your child's source of education," reflected the new school's principal.[25]

Claymont had undergone many changes over the centuries. Its origins were agricultural, as many early Delaware communities were. It slowly transformed into suburbia and a relaxation area for many Philadelphia families with wealth to spare. In the early 1900s, it became a community of industrial workers, many of whom worked at the steel plants.[26] Claymont would continue to evolve as its Catholic schools had changed. The steel mill was shuttered in 2013, with 375 workers losing their jobs.[27] Brookview Apartments, seen as a model neighborhood in the 1950s, became known for its crime rather than its community. By 2005, it was primarily a low-income housing complex and was demolished to make room for the Darley Green townhome development. Some local leaders thought prospective buyers were crazy, but the project persisted.[28] "We removed the single biggest stigma in Claymont when we tore down the Brookview Apartments," said Don Robitzer, an officer with the original developer. "They were in disrepair, unoccupied and a portion was burnt down."[29]

2

ARCHMERE AND DELAWARE

Joe spotted the grounds and buildings of Archmere Academy from his back bedroom window in the Brookview Apartments. Some might have thought of Archmere as an odd landmark in the steel town of Claymont, a short distance from the mills that employed many. For Joe, it was the first ornate mansion he had ever seen, and he was fixated, staring at it for hours. Later, he practiced Catholic Youth Organization football on its grounds. "When I was ten, getting to Archmere seemed enough," Joe later wrote. "I'd sit and stare out my bedroom window and dream of the day I would walk through the front doors and take my spot in that seat of learning."[30]

That day came, thanks in part to a summer of physical labor on the campus. Tuition was $300 a year, or about $3,200 today. (The school's actual yearly tuition at the time of this writing is $34,100.)[31] Joe was determined to attend, despite the tuition being outside the Bidens' budget, and he lined up a summer work-study job. From 8:00 a.m. to 4:00 p.m., he washed windows, painted fences and pulled weeds, earning his cherished spot each day.[32]

The Patio, as the school's main home was originally known, was built by John Jakob Raskob, a financier and businessman. Designed in the Italian Renaissance style by architects Clay McClure and Alexander James Harper of Wilmington, the Patio was based on fifteenth-century Florence residences. Built from Kentucky limestone for an initial estimate of $411,000, it sits on a concrete foundation and features eight limestone chimneys. An interior two-story courtyard was built with a mosaic "A" in the center, surrounded by Corinthian columns and covered by a stained-glass skylight, originally

Joe, Beau, Hunter and Ashley Biden all attended Archmere Academy, founded as an all-boys boarding school on the former estate of DuPont executive John J. Raskob. *Rachel Kipp.*

able to be retracted into the third floor. The second floor housed the Raskob family's bedrooms and servants' quarters; both his and hers suites contained fireplaces. A garage, also built from limestone, was connected to the house via a tunnel that ran underground; the garage featured a full repair shop, a car wash and laundry, as well as sleeping quarters for servants. Later buildings were added after the Norbertine Order purchased the property in 1932, with the Patio serving as an instructional building, student dorm, teacher housing and location for special occasions.[33]

To Raskob, the Patio was both a monument to its Italian heritage and a home, and the residence was its foremost purpose. In 1917, while the home was being designed and built, Raskob wrote to his architects:

> *Please keep in mind that we have a large family of children who are going to grow up in this house and that it is very important to have things in such shape as will result in their always feeling that it is a home and not a cold, formal and stately castle which they would like to get away from.*[34]

The property bore the name Archmere starting in 1873 upon its purchase by George Troutman, named for an arch that the trees along the Delaware

River had formed. Troutman's daughter sold the seventy-acre property to Raskob after her father's death for $27,000. The family moved in but found the existing mansion house too small for their family, so they built the Patio.

Raskob was a numbers man in the DuPont organization whose financial genius led him to highly powerful positions leading General Motors and the Democratic Party. Born in New York State, Raskob studied accounting at a local business college. That led him to a steel firm in Nova Scotia, and then he gained employment as a bookkeeper and personal secretary to Pierre S. du Pont. Raskob's influence allowed him to rise to the position of company treasurer in 1909, after he helped guide the company's growth to control a majority of black powder and dynamite production in the United States. He later advised the du Ponts to purchase $25 million of GM stock, which led to the auto manufacturer handing over control to DuPont. Raskob was named chairman of the GM finance committee, and created GMAC, making cars affordable for the first time for many Americans.[35] He became a millionaire by age forty.[36]

After corporate changes, Raskob set his sights on politics and became a chairman of the Democratic Party, helping steer Al Smith's losing campaign against Herbert Hoover in 1928. (The campaign was run out of Archmere.) He later combined forces with Smith to erect the Empire State Building in New York City and found himself on the losing side of presidential politics in 1932 as a foe of Franklin Delano Roosevelt.

Raskob sold the property in 1932, as Archmere was becoming surrounded by new development. The Norbertines, based out of DePere, Wisconsin, met with Raskob at the 1932 Democratic National Convention in Chicago and settled on a price. The new school opened on September 14, 1932, a mere seventy-odd days later.[37]

Biden later wrote of his entrance to the hallowed halls:

> *The bus rolled down past the wrought-iron fence (which gleamed with fresh black paint), through the big stone pillars that formed the front gate, and down the yellow-brick road to Raskob's mansion where the windows shined in the morning light.*

The school was rigorous and Catholic-centered. In his first semester, Joe had two periods of Latin per day. He gasped when he walked into the dark-wood, book-lined library—"I thought I'd died and gone to Yale"—but Archmere also marked a period of intense challenge for Joe over his longtime stutter. Nicknamed "Joe Impedimenta," he took the test earnestly,

The Archmere name comes from the natural arch formed by trees along the Delaware River. Raskob, a financial genius, was a millionaire by his fortieth birthday. *Delaware Public Archives.*

standing in front of the mirror in his room and practicing by reciting Yeats and Emerson. By the time of his graduation in 1961, Joe, as senior class president, delivered a welcome to parents and friends without stuttering once. "It was the final confirmation that the stutter was not going to hold me back," Joe recalled.[38]

Despite working hard, Joe wasn't a complete grind. "No one would ever accuse him of being an outstanding student," said Joe's friend and classmate David Walsh.[39] He was a B student, said later headmaster Michael Marinelli. "He wasn't the bookworm, but he certainly could gather around people and get things done."[40] Joe played football, winning special acclaim for his ability to score. A Wilmington newspaper described his last game thusly: "Halfback Joe Biden, who is high up in the state scoring race, was the standout in his final game. He tallied three touchdowns on runs of 4, 12 and 45 yards." That senior year team finished the season undefeated.[41] That Archmere football team of 1960 held several reunions at Joe's houses, in 1985 (twenty-fifth) and 2000 (fortieth).[42]

There were also rumors of Joe streaking through the parking lot.[43] Joe spent time looking out for the younger students and once took an underclassman to the prom along with his date. "I'd pick up some freshman who was being razzed and give him a ride home, maybe stop by the Charcoal Pit so he could be seen with me," he said.[44] Joe dated a friend of his sister Valerie's starting at Archmere and continuing through his sophomore year in college.[45]

As a parent of three children who attended Archmere, Joe was also involved, including helping decorate the gym for prom in 1988. "He was always himself, but when he came here he was an alum, he was a parent," recalled Bill Gehrman, who attended the school along with Beau and Hunter and was later the director of institutional advancement.[46]

College for Joe occurred at the University of Delaware, which he entered in the fall of 1961. He chose political science and history as his majors.[47] There were pranks and hijinks, as he was dinged for using a fire extinguisher on the dorm director.[48] Joe joined the football team, as he had done at Archmere. By one account, Joe Sr. made him quit the team after first semester grades were released; in another version of the story, Joe quit to save precious time commuting to see his girlfriend in New York State.[49]

The University of Delaware was and is a respectable and respected state school, in recent years working to raise its profile, especially in the STEM fields. Its roots trace back to a "free school" founded by a Presbyterian minister named Francis Alison in Chester County, Pennsylvania, in 1743. It moved to Newark and became the Academy of Newark, Newark College, Delaware College and, finally, the University of Delaware in 1921. Women were not permanently admitted until the latter half of the 1800s; a Women's College was formed in 1914 and was folded fully into the university in 1945.

The university had solid working relationships with Governors Elbert Carvel, who served as a trustee, and Caleb Boggs, who was an alumnus. The school was undergoing massive growth and change during Biden's time as a student. There were 3,600 undergraduates in 1961, growing to 6,500 by 1967. Women were elected student government presidents in 1957 and 1968. In 1967, the University of Delaware began its two-year "parallel program" in Georgetown, allowing students to save money and transfer north if desired. Student life was still restrictive, however. A dress code and a ban on cars were in place through 1967. Women were not permitted to study in the library while wearing pants, except during exam times.[50]

Joe spent his time plugging away, having fun and dating. He was elected president of his freshman class, beating four other contenders.[51] "He probably never studied as hard as other people did," said Joe's freshman year roommate and fellow football player Donald Brunner.[52] Biden graduated in 1965, with his plans taking him next to law school.

One thing that never affected Joe was excessive drinking—or drinking of any sort. He was a teetotaler at the University of Delaware and has stayed

The University of Delaware is now home to the Biden School of Public Policy and Administration, located in Graham Hall. *Dan Shortridge.*

that way for the rest of his life, seeing alcohol and other chemicals as a "crutch." Valerie also says she and her siblings all saw the broken hearts and pain that came from alcohol abuse while growing up. "There was nothing good that came from it," she said. "I believe, as does my brother, that you are genetically predisposed to it; genes will out, so I didn't want to take the chance." Beau was similarly inclined; he drank socially but quit at age thirty.[53]

In 1962, Joe took a summer job lifeguarding at a city-run pool in Wilmington, at Prices Run in Brown-Burton-Winchester Park. It was an eye-opening, consciousness-raising experience for Joe, as he was the only white lifeguard in a staff of twelve. His coworkers were all Black, and it was the first time both types of young men had the real opportunity to learn from each other—on the pool deck and on the basketball court. "I was a fascination to everybody at Prices Run," Joe recalled. Some of the people, he said, had never talked in-depth to a white person.[54]

"It was the first time I got to know well and became good friends with all of these inner-city Black guys, all of whom were college students at historically Black colleges," Joe said. "They'd ask me questions like 'What

During one summer in college, Biden lifeguarded at the Prices Run Pool, which was later named after him. *Dan Shortridge.*

do white girls do? Where do you live?' It was almost like we were exchange students." One coworker asked him if he owned a five-gallon gasoline can, explaining that it was a necessity when traveling to see relatives in North Carolina, as most gas stations wouldn't let Black travelers fill up their tanks. These conversations were critical for Joe as he was coming out of white Irish Catholic schools and communities.[55]

"I wanted to get more involved," he said later. "I'd turn on the television and I'd see and listen to Dr. King and others, but I didn't know any Black people. So, I wanted to work here."

In the summer of 2017, the city of Wilmington renamed the Prices Run Pool the Joseph R. Biden Jr. Aquatic Center in honor of the former vice president. Biden climbed up into a lifeguard's chair, spread his arms wide and grinned.[56] "The neighborhood's always had my back. And God willing, I've always had your back, and I'll always have it as long as I'm around."[57]

3

STARTING A FAMILY AND A CAREER

Near the end of his time at the University of Delaware, Joe traveled to the Bahamas for spring break 1964. That was where he met Neilia Hunter, and it was love at first sight. "When I got back to Delaware," Joe recalled, "I stopped by our house in Mayfield instead to deliver the news. Val said I started yelling as soon as I opened the door, before I even walked across the threshold."

"Val! Val! C'mere. I found her," Joe hollered.

"Found who?" his sister replied.

"I met the girl I'm going to marry."

As a sign of Joe's commitment to Neilia, he quit the football team to free up his weekends for the commute to New York State, where she was a student at Syracuse University. "I'm not playing," he remembered telling the coach. "See, I met this girl, and she's at Syracuse—" The coach promptly hung up.[58]

The two dated, and after his graduation from the University of Delaware, Joe made his way to Syracuse Law School in the fall of 1965. There, he studied the law, met lifelong friend Jack Owens and considered his future path.[59] He also worked as a substitute teacher part time.[60]

After graduating from Syracuse University in 1964, Neilia taught English in Syracuse City Schools, at Bellevue Heights. She stood up for kids who were being bullied and was a listener for others; her students said she was a teacher highly in demand. Student Patricia Cowin Wojenski said that Neilia "must have seen something in me which, I don't know, what it was, that she felt that she needed to be in my life, and I really appreciated that."

When Neilia and Joe moved, they became pen pals, and she always wrote him back. Wojenski later went on to work at Bellevue.[61]

Delaware almost didn't get Joe as its senator. While in law school, he was thinking about running for office in New York and wrote a paper about the Republican congressman from Neilia's district as a way of exploring the prospect. But he still talked about running for office from Delaware. He was hedging his bets and trying to figure out where he would best fit.[62]

Yet after law school and some contemplation, Joe and Neilia moved to Delaware. He got some early career advice from Judge Bill Quillen, a member of Harvard's class of '59 whose family owned Quillen Brothers Ford. Joe Sr., who was then working as a car dealer, asked Quillen if he would meet with Joe Jr.[63]

"Joe's a sparkler," said Quillen, who would later serve on the Court of Chancery and the Delaware Supreme Court and was the Democratic nominee for governor in 1984. "My impression was, 'This guy's good. He would be good before a jury.' He was a little less talkative than usual, because he was trying to figure out something." Quillen suggested that Joe look more closely at Delaware for his law career. "I argued for Delaware strongly. It's the greatest place to practice law in the country. It's small. We've got the best of both worlds. We've got the usual business, and we've got the corporate business, and if you go to New York, you don't know what the hell you're going for."[64]

Joe came to Delaware. He and Neilia settled into a small yellow farmhouse that they rented on Marsh Road.[65] The children quickly came along, and Neilia taught at St. Catherine of Sienna and had plans to earn a higher degree and teach at the university level.[66]

Joe passed the bar exam in November 1968, and he and his fellow new Delaware attorneys were admitted to the bar in December at ceremonies in the supreme court chambers.[67] They were then invited to a reception at Woodburn, the governor's mansion in Dover, by Governor Charles Terry.[68]

Quillen gave Joe a reference to a firm called Prickett, Ward, Burt & Sanders and partner Rod Ward, who happened to be Quillen's college roommate.[69] The firm had been started decades earlier with a solo practitioner, William Sharp Prickett, who set up shop in Delaware in 1888. Located in a series of buildings along Wilmington's King Street, the firm's holdings include the distinguished Captain Thomas Starr House.[70] The house was built in the early 1800s by stonecutter Michael Van Kirk, who sold it to waterman Jacob Starr in 1806. Jacob's son, the eponymous Captain Starr, owned ships that ferried products along the East Coast. By 1954, William Prickett Sr. had bought the house for his law firm, then called Prickett & Prickett.[71]

Joe was hired but didn't last long at the corporate law firm. After a civil trial in which a partner had argued for negligence on the part of an injured worker—casting the blame on the employee—Biden called it quits. He begged off lunch with Rod Ward, and "by the time I got to the center of Rodney Square, I had decided to quit Prickett, Ward."[72] He walked across the street to the public defender's office and got a part-time job in a role far removed from the insurance defense business; 90 percent of his clients there were Black residents of Wilmington's East Side.[73]

One of Biden's early cases as a public defender that caught the attention of the news was a cattle-rustling case brought against a Wilmington fisherman. Biden's client had hauled the cow into his pickup at a Townsend farm, driven it to the Hartly area and sold it. Biden pleaded for leniency, saying his client had been having a difficult financial time and that he was allowed to plead guilty to a lesser charge of petty larceny. He was, in Biden's words, "not a very adept criminal."[74] Another case involved a tractor-trailer driver who was carrying a load of frozen seafood but halted in Delaware for a "week's drunk," in Biden's words. The food was stolen when he left the trailer unlocked.[75]

Biden later joined the firm of Aerenson & Balick doing civil litigation while also working for the public defender's office.[76] Partner Sid Balick was a mentor who also whetted Joe's appetite for politics. (Balick had run for state attorney general and would later serve in the Delaware General Assembly.)[77] During one conversation, "he [Joe] suggested I run for governor," Balick recalled. "I sensed he really wanted to talk about himself." Joe asked if it was OK to run for office while working at the firm. Balick said it would be fine if his campaign didn't involve conflicts, and he was only working at the firm part time. He later encouraged Biden to make his first bid for public office. Joe would later go on to form a small law firm with one of his best friends from Archmere, David Walsh, in 1969.[78]

Joe's cases included a civil lawsuit filed against the Penn Central Railroad on behalf of two sets of drivers who were injured when, Biden claimed, the trains drove too fast through crossings without gates or lights and the engineers did not blow their whistles.[79] With Walsh, Joe also represented ten couples who claimed they were not paid overtime while working as houseparents and counselors at the Governor Bacon Health Center in Delaware City. The couples were asking for $438,000 in unpaid overtime costs—equivalent to $3.4 million today.[80]

Balick said Biden was better with the clients than with finessing the arguments in case law. "As a lawyer he was very good with people. If

Before getting into politics, Biden was an attorney for Aerenson & Balick. He called Sid Balick, who died in 2017, his "first true mentor." *Dan Shortridge.*

somebody had a legal problem, he'd put his arm around them and comfort them and they loved it. But writing briefs wasn't his forte."[81]

"I've had a lot of mentors—nuns in grade school, priests in high school and professors in college and law school, but Sid Balick was my first true mentor aside from my own parents and grandparents," Joe recalled after Balick's death in 2017. "His family became ours. He was a man of honor and character."[82]

Along the way, Biden's soft spot for animals came out. One day in March 1969, he found a wounded St. Bernard dog sitting outside of the Farmers Bank building, where his office was located. He took it home, dubbed it Governor and called the newspaper to match it with an owner. Later that day, the owner contacted Biden and identified the dog, named Sinbad.[83]

During this time in the late 1960s, America was struggling with the war in Vietnam, and Delaware was dealing with the civil rights movement. The assassination of Dr. Martin Luther King Jr. led to protests and unrest in Wilmington, and Governor Charles Terry responded by ordering the national guard into the city.[84] "Every day I went to work at Prickett, Ward, I walked by six-foot-tall uniformed white soldiers carrying rifles. Apparently

Governor Charles Terry, who ordered the national guard into Wilmington for a lengthy occupation, also led the Delaware Supreme Court as chief justice. *Delaware Public Archives.*

they were there to protect me," said Biden. The mostly Black communities in Wilmington were angry at the guard "rat patrols" and worried about their children coming home safely.[85]

Terry was a traditional politician in nontraditional times who severely misjudged the changing mores. A judge by vocation, who served from 1938 to 1964, including time spent as a supreme court chief justice, Terry served one term as governor and was unseated by Russell Peterson.[86]

Peterson could not have been a clearer contrast to Terry. A chemist by training—and a Republican—he focused his political strength on the environment, passing the transformational Coastal Zone Management Act into law.[87] ("To hell with Shell," Peterson said, providing fodder for anti-

Governor Russell Peterson (*second from left, shaking hands*) struggled to overcome a state budget deficit that darkened his most successful moment, the passing of the Delaware Coastal Zone Act. *Delaware Public Archives.*

refinery buttons.) He also oversaw a transition from a commission form of state government to a strong governor cabinet form. But the very day that he signed the Coastal Zone Management Act, which should have been a celebration, he was forced to announce a deficit of $5 million, about 2 percent of the state's budget, due to errors in the revenue forecasts. "Peterson had gone from perhaps the proudest moment in his political life to his worst," Cohen wrote. He was booed at the high school blue-gold football game over the summer.[88]

Biden was a Peterson fan, partly for his activist approach and partly for him pulling the guard out of Wilmington. "There was no greater act than that first official one," he said after Peterson's death in 2011.[89]

Peterson was unseated in 1972 by Democrat Sherman Tribbitt, who had previously served as lieutenant governor and speaker of the House.[90] Like Peterson, he struggled to right the financial ship, but he also faced challenges. A ship struck a railroad bridge across the C&D Canal, the Delaware City Oil Refinery was threatened by a shutdown and Farmers Bank came close to collapse. "God threw everything into one administration," said Tribbitt's secretary and future governor Ruth Ann Minner.[91] Like Terry and Peterson before him, Tribbitt served just one term before being given the boot.

4

THE FIRST CAMPAIGN

Biden became involved in Democratic politics while serving as part of a reform-minded group called the Democratic Forum and being elected its vice president.[92] Still, his first campaign was not in his master plan. He wanted to get into politics, but the county council did not excite him. Land use, zoning and minor matters were not Joe's forte. He told that to John Daniello, then a member of the council and a future state Democratic chairman, who approached him about being a candidate in 1970. His passions were foreign relations and the deep tracks of history; local politics was not his thing.[93] But he was talked into running and ran a solid campaign.

The Fourth District was a new one, formed after redistricting. Joe put many hours in on the campaign trail in Stanton, Newport and Elsmere, then Democratic strongholds, going door to door. He also put in time in Republican areas, knocking and talking in communities similar to Mayfield and Brookview, where he had grown up. "I knew how to talk to them," Joe reflected later.[94]

Biden was critical of county government and its trend of increasing taxes while decreasing services or holding them flat, pointing out the elevated cost of police while seeing the crime rate also rise.[95] On crime, he called for expanding the criminal division, forming special teams with specialized training, hiring a full-time county police director and building better cooperation between state and county officers behind the scenes, including new records and equipment. "The people of the county could understand this need for more money if they were, in turn, receiving better services and better protection," he said. "The people are paying more and getting less."[96] He also proposed reorganizing the county's public works agency to improve garbage pickup, saying it should reduce costs, which were two to three times higher for residents in the unincorporated areas of the county than they were for residents of Wilmington or Newport.[97] And he called for broader-scale public housing, with twenty-five- to thirty-unit sites around the county with full-time directors living on site. "Everybody's opposed to public housing—no one wants it in their backyard, but [expletive], if you have a moral obligation to provide it, provide it—but spread the load around," he said.[98]

His opponent was Larry Messick, age forty-eight. A World War II veteran of D-Day, Messick, like Biden, was not a Delaware native but part of the "come-here" trend. Born in New Jersey, he was drafted into the army and later played in General George Patton's band. Though he once had plans for medical school, he returned to the United States to earn his degrees from Temple University and the University of Pennsylvania, focusing on education. He became a music teacher and led the Wilmington All-City Orchestra, eventually retiring in 1977. In 1970, he was teaching a real estate course at Brandywine Junior College. Messick's platform included creating a county housing authority and instituting policies "that will not create new ghettos." He later worked as a homebuilder, played in a Dixieland band and served as a chairman of the county board of elections.[99] (Messick and his wife, Blanche, were proud supporters of Joe Biden and served as leaders of Republicans for Biden when he ran for the Senate.)[100]

Neilia was Joe Biden's secret weapon in his county council race and his first Senate race. During her studies at Syracuse, she was homecoming queen and on the dean's list and later earned a master's in education. She worked with children with disabilities. A Republican from New York's Finger Lakes, she registered as a Democrat in Delaware. She once told a reporter of her parents' opposition to her and Joe's wedding: "I guess the only time I got in trouble with my parents was when I wanted to marry Joe," she said. "He was Irish Catholic and we were Scotch Presbyterian, but they liked him too much to say no." Later, when her small family was compared to the Kennedys of Massachusetts, she said wryly, "I don't know the Kennedys, but I don't think they could be half as great as the Bidens."[101]

Indeed, her down-to-earth nature was one of the things that made Neilia such an advantage for Joe. "I'm not worried about being the lonely political wife. If we can survive six years, we can survive anything," she once said. On another occasion, she spoke of the lack of glamor and conveniences on the campaign trail: "There never was any place or time to change. We'd go from an informal function to something formal and many times I'd just change in the car and tell (the kids) not to look." Joe himself said there were two primary decision-makers in the campaign, him and Neilia. "She was the brains. And she also prevented me from blowing my top when I got angry late in the going."[102]

Initial voting from high school students at McKean High School favored Messick, beating Biden 61 percent to 39 percent.[103] In actual election results in November, the year was generally a glum one for statewide Democrats (Daniello lost a bid for Congress to Pete du Pont), but Joe won the Fourth District on the New Castle County Council by 2,381 votes.[104]

Just days after the election, Delaware Democrats were promoting Biden for higher office. "He has all the qualifications for a great future in government," said state party chairman Henry Topel. "Joe Biden is one of the most promising young men the Democratic Party in Delaware has ever seen." A reporter painted a portrait using phrases once used to describe women during a bygone age: "He's about to become 28, and his eyes sparkle blue, and his teeth shine when he smiles, his cheeks glow, and his body is still boyishly slim," reporter Jane Harriman wrote. "And, one suspects, when his hair has receded, and his frame thickened with maturity, the charm will only increase." For her part, Neilia imagined her husband's career rising to the chambers and dark robes of the U.S. Supreme Court.[105]

After the election, Biden was critical of the party leadership: "There must be more sophisticated ways to attack the fact that Republicans have more money than we do," he declared. "We have been consistently foolish for six years.…There is a whole new purview, old coalitions have been demolished. Why have we allowed the Republicans to steal the Democratic banner of progressive government?"[106]

The county council was not glamorous, but it netted Biden quite a few headlines, especially in northern Delaware, the state's population center, which raised his name recognition for his statewide bid. He would have a title in front of his name and a platform—and results—behind him. One of those key issues was raising concerns and introducing a rezoning ordinance about a new Shell refinery near Smyrna, which bolstered his standing with environmentalists.[107] "We already had enough experience with on large petrochemical complex in the county," he said, referring to the Delaware City refinery run by Getty.[108]

Joe also used part of his county salary to open an office for constituent concerns, located a few doors down from his law offices on King Street in

Wilmington. "I just don't want to be put in a position of ever having it said that I've reneged on my campaign promises," he said.[109] And he weighed in on solutions to sewer problems, speaking "longest and loudest on the matter," a reporter said, while declaring he would not vote for any rezoning "until we've decided how it's going to develop."[110] On roads, he urged wider adoption of mass transit, warning that state highway plans would cover northern New Castle County with concrete that would force parents in 1990 to "take your kids to the park in a helicopter."[111]

5

ROAD TO THE SENATE

With the county council under his belt and a small amount of name recognition, Joe turned his eyes to the U.S. Senate. That was a tremendous leap for a young attorney who was not yet old enough to be sworn in, but Joe took the leap.

The office was then held by U.S. senator James Caleb Boggs, known as Cale, a political powerhouse and the strongman of Delaware Republican Party politics. A lawyer by trade, he was a fellow graduate of the University of Delaware who then went to Georgetown Law School.

A World War II Bronze Star winner and armored cavalry colonel in the European theater, Boggs returned to Delaware and became a state family court judge in 1946. A year later, he was elected to the U.S. House of Representatives, serving until 1953. Boggs then ran for governor in the 1952 election, sending Governor Elbert Carvel home to Laurel for a few years, and he won his second term in 1956.[112] Boggs hadn't lost a race since 1946.[113] Perhaps most critically, as Valerie would recall, Boggs had held elected office for twenty-five years; Joe was just twenty-nine years old.[114]

News Journal columnist Al Cartwright laid out the challenge facing Biden in a 1972 column. Boggs had won just shy of six hundred thousand votes in the races he'd won so far, Cartwright noted. Boggs's prior opponents called him "a splendid politician" (Carl McGuigan, 1948), "such a nice guy" and "everybody's friend" (Tyler McConnell, 1956). "If they had a congeniality prize in Washington, Boggs would have retired it by now," Cartwright concluded.

Biden's pitch was simple, Cartwright said: "Biden maintains the man's depth stops there. He argues that the only thing Boggs has shaken as a senator is hands."[115]

Boggs was fundamentally a product of a different era: born in 1909, when William Howard Taft was president, and graduated college during the Great Depression.[116] Biden saw an opening to seize his advantage—and a path to his victory. "He's tired," he told skeptical friends. "Boggs!" his friends said. "You're [expletive] crazy."[117]

In March 1971, the *Evening Journal* ran a series about the failures of the Delaware Democratic Party in the last three voting cycles: failures of leadership, a failure to shift to modern political tactics and a failure to focus on suburban New Castle County. One more item appealed to hopefuls of Biden's sort: "a failure to develop new, attractive candidates." Biden himself was quoted in the article as a critic of party leadership. "All the Republicans did in the State of Delaware was to co-opt the Kennedy thing and run with it," he said. "I ran as Joe Biden, who is brighter, more intelligent and better researched than my opponent.…It seems to me there is a change in attitude in this state toward elected officials. Minorities and other vested interests are sick and tired of hollow promises."[118]

That summer, Delaware Democrats met in Dover for their off-year convention. Joe was staying at the Hub Motel at the corner of Loockerman Street, a roadside lodging establishment known for its bar and politicians.[119] He was standing at the sink, shaving in his underwear, when two men, Henry Topel, the state party chairman, and Elbert Carvel, the former governor, knocked on the door. "I asked their forbearance while I took a second to put on my pants," Joe said. The two men sat down on the motel room's twin beds and asked Joe to consider challenging Boggs and running for the U.S. Senate. Joe said he'd have to think about it, "and from that moment on I couldn't stop thinking about it," he wrote later.[120] The convention was a fairly raucous and disunited one, with a reorganized party structure that made some members upset, but Topel continued in his role, and Biden went forth inspired.[121]

His county council district, by that point, had been redrawn by Republicans, moving from 55 percent Republican—tough but winnable—to more than 60 percent GOP, an untenable prospect for any Democrat. "I had no place to go," Joe said later. "It was up or out."

Opposite: A young Cale Boggs, shown here in 1941, served in the U.S. Army in Europe. He would serve as a member of Congress, a governor and a U.S. senator. *Delaware Public Archives.*

Left: Cale Boggs sits at a desk in Washington. He only ran for a third term in 1972 at the urging of President Richard Nixon. *Delaware Public Archives.*

So, in 1971, the Biden campaign—actually, the Biden family—began a quiet run. "It was coffee under the radar," Joe recalled, inspired by John F. Kennedy's neighborhood teas during his first congressional campaign. They would begin bright and early at 8:00 a.m. A small horde of Bidens (Jean, Neilia, Valerie and Joe, plus his children, Beau, Hunter and Naomi) would descend on the homes of volunteer hosts for small, intimate gatherings. After forty-five minutes, they would leapfrog to the next house, doing up to ten coffee stops each day. On downstate coffee days, they wouldn't return home until close to midnight, the kids and Neilia sleeping in the station wagon. The days were long, but they worked, connecting the nascent Biden campaign to hundreds of people every day for them to hear his message and for him to hear their concerns. The quiet effort lasted throughout the fall of 1971 and into early 1972, laying the groundwork and raising Joe's profile and name recognition as he prepared for the biggest bet of his life.[122]

Publicly, he was signaling his intentions as well. In September, he told the *Evening Journal* that he was considering a campaign against Boggs. "Biden could give one hell of a race," observed New Castle County Democratic chairman Edward F. Peterson. "He's young, but the party needs more young candidates. I believe in going with a winner."[123]

Biden, along with future governor Sherman Tribbitt, were widely sought out at a Democratic get-together in Sussex County that month. Joe was also mentioned as a potential candidate for Congress against Pete du Pont if Boggs were to retire. "Despite Biden's apparent popularity in Sussex, he just isn't the Sussex County–type candidate (too young, too liberal, too quick, etc.)," the *Evening Journal*'s Sussex bureau chief Ron Williams wrote. "On the other hand, maybe Sussex County Democrats have realized it's 1971 and that there is a New Castle County and a city of Wilmington."[124]

Against the backdrop of the time, Biden's youth was a motivating factor rather than a negative one. "Mr. Biden has more than age going for him," the *Morning News* editorial writers concluded. "He is a joyous campaigner, his whole family joining in his effort. He is an articulate man who chooses his battleground carefully as a minority voice on the County Council."[125]

The Senate campaign's formal kickoff was held at the Hotel DuPont in downtown Wilmington, a traditional Republican location for political and other events. Known as "Wilmington's front door" since it opened in 1913, the twenty-seven-story hotel has been a place to see and be seen by generations of Delawareans, business leaders and attorneys. Its famed Green Room restaurant was the prime dining spot for special occasions. The hotel's public spaces have held birthday parties, weddings, proms and community organization meetings for decades. One group, Wilmington's Rotary Club, held its meetings there for nearly one hundred years.[126]

As suggested by its name, the Hotel DuPont was founded by the DuPont company, based in its downtown Wilmington headquarters. DuPont had moved to its new Wilmington offices in 1907 from its Brandywine Works north of Delaware's largest city. The hotel, DuPont imagined, would house business executives traveling to Wilmington and other leaders who insisted on a world-class lodging and dining venue. Pierre S. du Pont led the hotel as its president, and John J. Raskob, whose estate became Archmere Academy, was its secretary-treasurer. The hotel opened in 1913 with 150 rooms. Its vast array of silverware included 7,272 pieces, 495 dozen spoons and forks and 100 dozen knives, and dishes for every conceivable purpose, as one newspaper described: "coffee pots, chocolate pots, tea pots, toureens and plates, meat dishes, covers for meat dishes, wine coolers and stands, waiters, cash and card trays, mustard pots, ice-bowls, compotes, finger bowls, caviar dishes" and beyond. In later years, the Gold Ballroom, the Brandywine Room, and the Green Room restaurant were added on. Except for a short

The Biden family during Joe's 1972 Senate campaign (*left to right*): Hunter, Neilia, Naomi, Joe and Beau. This postcard photograph featured a Neilia chicken recipe on the back. *Delaware Public Archives.*

period from 1927 to 1933, the hotel was run by DuPont until 2017. DuPont examined selling or closing the hotel in 1955 but decided to invest in giving it a more modern look and feel instead. Later, the hotel also trained its staff in the basics of Japanese to make guests from that country feel welcome.[127]

The hotel's art displays include paintings by Howard Pyle, three generations of Wyeths and Ed Loper Sr., all hanging in various rooms. It has hosted countless VIPs and celebrities, including Presidents Harry S. Truman and John F. Kennedy, along with Amelia Earhart, Duke Ellington, Ginger Rogers, Jesse Jackson and Katharine Hepburn.

In 2017, DuPont sold its hotel business to Wilmington-based Buccini/Pollin, a large northern Delaware developer that has come to dominate the city's skyline with new and renovated buildings and ventures. The company had previously agreed to purchase the DuPont building, which came with the hotel, offices and a theater space, from Chemours, a DuPont spinoff. Its 217 rooms would remain as hotel rooms, and the company would continue running it as a hotel. Former Hotel DuPont manager William Sullivan said the public spaces of the hotel were in amazing shape and would just need a usual eight- to ten-year refresh. "The hotel, as people recognize it, will largely stay the same," said Buccini/Pollin executive Michael Hare.

Still, the sale sparked wistful reflection on the part of many. Hotel retiree Tom Hannum, who had worked there for thirty-three years as an executive

The Hotel DuPont in Wilmington has been the site of many Biden campaign events over the years, including his 1972 kickoff and election night victory party. *Delaware Public Archives.*

chef and food and beverage manager, called it Delaware's "center of the universe" for big events of all varieties. "It was a special place to have special events," he said. Sullivan said Buccini/Pollin was a good choice because the company is headquartered locally. "Its workers have had their proms there and attended countless weddings and social events there. This is the best possible outcome," he said.[128]

On March 20, Biden stepped up to the lectern in the hotel's storied DuBarry Room and spoke for more than forty minutes.[129] He spoke of unity and common ground: "We must have public officials who will stand up and tell the people exactly what they think….We have often allowed our differences to prevail among us….But all our differences hardly measure up to the values we all hold in common."[130]

Biden was polling thirty points behind Cale Boggs, needed to raise $150,000 and was openly aiming for a miracle. "If I were a bookie, I'd give five-to-one odds right now that Boggs will be reelected," he told people. Voters would sometimes attend Joe's events and think that he was the son of the Biden running.[131]

Delaware had recently dropped "straight-ticket" voting, which helped Biden in November. The former system featured a single lever that allowed voters to choose all Republicans or all Democrats with a single *thunk*. The new system would require some thought and individual consideration of each position, allowing for split-ticket voting, contest by contest. That would have the effect of separating Biden from the top of his party's ticket, U.S senator George McGovern. McGovern went down in flames that year; Biden came out on top.[132]

To boost Democratic energy, the Bidens went to work. Ahead of the state convention in June at Dover Central Middle School, they assembled a "Biden Band" from high school marching bands and met in the parking lot. "When Joe's name was put into nomination that Saturday morning, we burst through the auditorium, drums beating, horns blazing, chanting, 'Go, Joe, Joe, Joe!' That band led us as we wove through the aisles out of their seats to join us in a snake dance. It turned into one big conga line," Valerie recalled.[133]

After the Hotel DuPont announcement, the Bidens launched what would become a multidecade tradition, the three-county tour, kicking off campaigns in New Castle, Kent and Sussex Counties. Democrats had typically done just one event, usually holding it at a fire hall. "No statewide candidate had ever done this before," Valerie remembered. "Three announcements, three crowds, three press conferences." Instead of driving, Joe set off in the copilot seat of a Piper Cub with Beau on his lap, two small planes following with the rest of the clan.[134] They went first to Sussex and then to Kent. The spectacle was impressive, with hundreds turning out. "Whatever else people thought about Joe, he no longer looked like a total amateur," Valerie said later.[135]

Rich Heffron was a volunteer on the first Biden Senate campaign who went on to have a long career with the Delaware State Chamber of Commerce. "[Joe] was the Energizer Bunny. He'd never stop," Heffron said. "If you went to a high school football game on Saturday morning, he was there. If you went to the Acme, he was there. If you went to the Delaware football game in the afternoon, he was there. He had that smile, that grin; he was everybody's best friend."[136]

By March, some were taking note, including columnist Bill Frank. "Joe should realize a lot of people are seriously looking at him and evaluating him as a runner," Frank noted, but he went on to criticize Biden for not mentioning Vietnam or busing in his kickoff address.[137] Frank weighed in again in June: "I wouldn't ignore him. He has verve, spirit, empathy, enthusiasm. He's not bound by the old traditional rules of campaigning.… At times, Biden is impudent and downright impertinent. He's refreshing and has a good sense of humor—and he's got the Potomac fever real bad."

Still, the columnist concluded, "The truth is the only man who's going to ruin Biden's campaign will be Biden himself. He actually came out the other night and said he couldn't predict what he will say or do during the campaign." As for Boggs: "He's been campaigning for 25 years, more or less.…But he'll find this young opponent a rare treat. He's never been up against such a rival and for we who sit on the sidelines, it's going to be lots of fun."[138]

Neilia was as much a force in the campaign as Joe was. During drives, Neilia would steer the car with Joe riding shotgun. At red lights, Joe would leap out of the passenger seat, dash back to shake hands with passengers in the cars behind them and then sprint back to the station wagon before the light turned green.[139] At one Boggs campaign event held at the Hotel DuPont in mid-October, the candidate complained about a Biden campaign advertisement. Attending as a "tracker," following the opposing candidate to document slipups or gaffes, was Neilia Biden. Wilmington mayor Harry Haskell, a Republican, called out her presence.[140]

The campaign was strategized from the Bidens' living room in Sunday night meetings between Joe, Neilia, Valerie, the twenty-six-year-old campaign manager and Joe's brother Jimmy.[141] They set up a public headquarters on Wilmington's Market Street, located behind Joe's law office and filled with old DuPont furniture.[142] The first week in October brought new polling numbers—it was a dead heat, tied solid, up from thirty points down a few months prior. "The Delaware Republican Party had been so fixated on holding the governorship, they hadn't seen me coming," Joe recalled. "And Boggs' advisors had been telling him all along that the race was a lock and he didn't even have to leave Washington."[143]

Along the way, the campaign volunteers formed a bond. Biden would have them over to his house, swimming in the pool and playing games of touch football. "I guess we thought we were the Kennedys," said Heffron. "We were a bunch of kids. We were too stupid to think we couldn't win the race."[144]

In late October, Biden took a different approach in the last few days before the election, heading to Salisbury, Maryland, to cut television advertisements with customized messaging for upstate and downstate voters, focusing on the environment and emphasizing Boggs's long tenure over the changing decades. Reporter Norman Lockman, later a Pulitzer Price–winning columnist, called it the "dear old dad" approach. Biden also met with U.S. senator Lloyd Bentsen of Texas to talk about his successful campaign, turning out Senator Ralph Yarborough in the primary and sending Republican George Bush to a new job as ambassador to the United Nations. "I thought they would go after me where I'm vulnerable, really hit the 'young and inexperienced' bit. But they've not been logical," Biden confided. "Earlier, they could have really undressed me; now I've done my homework."[145]

Also in the closing days, Biden hammered home the theme of generational change while taking pains not to be overly critical of Boggs. One advertisement read: "In 1950 Cale Boggs hoped to make Americans safe from Stalin. In 1972 Joe Biden hopes to make Americans safe from criminals."[146] A similar message said, "Cale Boggs' generation dreamed of conquering polio. Joe Biden's generation dreams of conquering heroin."[147] Boggs's message was simple: "Delaware's Senator CALE BOGGS: He gets things done in Washington."[148] But that would not be enough this year.

At the start of the Biden campaign, Valerie played a trump card that would lead to claims of audacity on the Bidens' part. The Hotel DuPont was a traditional Republican gathering spot for campaign celebrations. But that April, Valerie strolled in and put a chit down for the Gold Ballroom for their election victory party. "We took their prize, and they didn't even notice until they strolled through, in September, to claim what they viewed as their birthright. You could hear the roar through the city: Biden did *what?*"[149]

There was financial support from some unexpected quarters: builders who wanted Joe off the county council after he opposed a few construction projects. In the final days of the campaign, Joe took out a $20,000 loan

Valerie and Joe at the White House in 2021. For decades, Valerie ran her brother's campaigns, organizing them like a political hawk. *White House.*

against his home known as North Star, cosigned by his finance chairman, Roy Wentz, to keep his radio spots on the air for the last week.[150]

The campaign also won strong support among Black communities in South Wilmington, thanks to Joe's time a decade earlier lifeguarding at Prices Run. He spoke at churches and union halls and dinners, and he got people to the polls in large numbers.[151] Just before the election, McGovern's running mate, Sargent Shriver, and his wife, Eunice Kennedy, visited for a campaign rally by torchlight, with Joe and Sargent eliciting the loudest cheers.[152]

In the end, the Biden clan pulled off the unthinkable—a political miracle—and won. They beat a twenty-five-year political veteran, a World War II hero who had held the top three positions in the state and who was blessed by President Nixon. Biden beat Boggs 116,006 to 112,844 (or a margin of 3,162 votes). It was slim, but it was enough.[153]

"I may be the worst senator," Biden told supporters on election night. "I may be the best, but I doubt it. I'm going to be a bit of a pest.…I hope I don't let you down." He would pick up enough votes in Brandywine Hundred, a suburban area, to make up the traditionally Republican difference in New Castle County. He graciously praised Boggs and his gentlemanly campaign. "It's a lot less joyous than I expected," Biden said. "I think of him and how he must feel after 26 years of faithful service." Boggs remained at home that night after many supporters left a Republican gathering on Philadelphia Pike.[154]

To some, Biden's victory was "total and complete shock," said top Biden aide and future senator Ted Kaufman. "I remember thinking, there is nothing that is impossible, because there was nothing I was involved in that was ever more impossible than having Joe Biden beat Cale Boggs. Nixon was at the top of the ticket, and this guy was 29 years old."[155]

A newspaper photograph from that night captured Neilia Biden speaking to the crowd, holding a microphone in her right hand and baby Naomi in her left. Neilia is grinning broadly. Naomi is sucking on her thumb, eyes wide.[156]

At the Hotel DuPont, Henry Topel got a call from U.S. senator Vance Hartke of Indiana. "I understand your man just won. What kind of a guy is he?" Hartke asked. Topel paused for a moment, and Hartke said, "You mean he wants to be president?" Topel laughed.[157]

After the election, Biden recalled a conversation with Neilia at their new North Star home. He talked in grandiose language about what the election meant. "I do, Neilia, I really do. I have great faith in the American people." The sharp-witted Neilia had a comeback. "Joey, I wonder how you would have felt if you lost."[158]

6

UNSPEAKABLE TRAGEDY

A few weeks after the election, Joe's family and friends celebrated his birthday at Piane Grill in Wilmington. It was partly a political event, too; Joe and Neilia cut the birthday cake in front of news cameras.[159] Times were looking great for the Biden family.

After the election, even amid all the bustle and chaos of setting up a Senate office, they quickly moved again, his parents back to their home on Woods Road and his family into North Star. They also found a small Colonial-style home in Washington, D.C., near Chevy Chase Circle, with an offer accepted on December 15. Joe said later:

> *It felt like we had finally arrived at the future we had so long envisioned. The Washington house was going to be nice, but North Star already felt like home—Thanksgivings and Christmases, Easters and birthdays and anniversaries, would all be celebrated at North Star. We planned on spending most weekends at North Star. When Beau and Hunt and Naomi thought of home, they'd think of North Star. And that Sunday night, with the children asleep over our heads, Neilia and I sat on our lone wing chair, in front of the warm glow of a fire, in our stone fireplace, in a moment of near perfect repose.[160]*

But in mid-December, a week before Christmas, everything changed.

Joe was in Washington, interviewing prospective staff members. Neilia had the kids at home—Beau, age four; Hunter, age three; and Naomi, age thirteen months. She had considered heading to Washington to join Joe that night—they were settling on a house there the next day—but stayed in Delaware instead.[161] She loaded the kids into the family station wagon to go buy a Christmas tree at Valley and Limestone Roads.[162] Naomi was riding in the front passenger's seat in a bassinet, Beau was behind Naomi and Hunter was behind Neilia.[163]

She stopped at the stop sign on Valley Road and then pulled through the intersection, where the car was instantly hit from the left by a truck coming down Limestone Road. The car spun for 150 feet before hitting an evergreen tree. The truck driver, Curtis C. Dunn, flipped his rig while trying to avoid the crash and got out and ran to the car to try to help.[164] Neilia and Naomi were pronounced dead; Beau had broken his left leg, and Hunter had a head injury.[165]

In the years to come, the family would call it "the accident."[166] That day, it was all they could do to hold it together for the kids. Joe flew back to Wilmington and headed straight into the hospital, looking directly ahead.[167]

As the horrible news spread, a radio announcer broke into the program with information on the crash. "It was profoundly unfair—to take a mother from her children; to take a daughter from her father," Jill recalled. "Joe Biden had everything, and in a horrible second, it was gone….That cold December evening, life truly stopped for a moment and I prayed for the Biden family. It was the only thing I could think to do."[168]

The burial of Neilia and Naomi was private, held at All Saints Cemetery.[169] All Saints was the second Catholic cemetery in Delaware, opened in 1958 to all denominations.[170] Neilia and Naomi's graves were later moved to St. Joseph's on the Brandywine after Joe Sr.'s death in 2002—"for the entire family to be together," Beau Biden told a reporter. "It's important that our family be together in all respects, to be at the church where we worship as a family."[171]

The burial was followed by a memorial service a few days later at Saint Mary Magdalen Catholic Church. Nearly seven hundred people joined the family in their grief at the service. Joe stood up and spoke. "Please don't be sad," he said. "I'm pretty proud of her. She had a principle—she treated everyone the same, and that worked both ways. Those who were poor, Black, minority, affluent or socially esteemed, she made no distinction among them.…I'm going to try to follow her example." Joe quoted John Milton, echoing the dark feelings inside: "I waked, she fled and day brought back my night." He thanked those who attended as they left the church.[172]

Neilia and Naomi were buried in All Saints Cemetery and reinterred at St. Joseph's on the Brandywine, shown above, after 2002. All Saints was the second Catholic cemetery in Delaware. *Delaware Public Archives.*

The grave marker for Neilia Hunter Biden and Naomi Christina Biden, who were killed in a car accident after Joe's Senate election victory in 1972. *Dan Shortridge.*

With Beau's passing, Hunter became the last survivor of the accident and the last repository of memories about his mother, whom the brothers called their mommy. He recalled later:

> *I was hyperaware of my mommy's death—and hyperaware of her absence. I loved hearing relatives' stories about her, holding tight to their portrayals of how special she was, how tough she was, how compassionate she was. They described her to me as smart, decisive, beautiful. The word I heard most often was* elegant, *as it related both to her demeanor and her physical appearance. She came across as something close to regal yet eminently approachable....I was not consciously aware, however, of how much her loss represented a missing piece of the family puzzle. While that hole was filled with something very special, what was lost was never recovered. It was if someone had torn a section from a painting and replaced it with a lovely likeness.*

The surviving Biden kids became symbols of survival and sorrow. "Beau and I became everyone's cousins, nephews, adopted children," recalled Hunter decades later. "The consequences of that crash impacted the entire state. Republican, Democrat—it didn't matter." Joe himself became imbued with the power of public tragedy, a "dashing young widower suddenly left with two toddlers."[173]

The media barely gave him the space and time to breathe or mourn. "All of a sudden I wasn't a person—I was a good story. And the reporters just would not leave me alone. Photographers snapped my picture as I walked out of the hospital, while reporters yelled their questions at me: 'Senator, how many stitches does Hunt have?' 'How many broken bones does Beau have?' 'How are you really doing, Senator?' 'How does it feel?'" Joe recalled later in his autobiography. "Well, it felt like Hell. I know they had a job to do, but they didn't seem willing to give me room to be human, to grieve." After that, Joe didn't take much time to cultivate relationships with or befriend reporters and instead focused on making his way out of the Capitol complex to get to Union Station on time.[174]

Still, every year, on December 18, the Biden family and a handful of friends gather for an anniversary to recall Neilia and Naomi. They go to the 7:00 a.m. mass at Saint Joseph's and then to Joe and Jill's house for a light breakfast. For many years, Joe, Beau and Hunter would visit the graves of their wife and mother, placing a wreath of white roses there.[175]

As it was for the Bidens, the date became a quiet moment in the truck driver, Dunn's, house. His family hid articles about the anniversary of the crash from him. He died in 1999, but his daughter wrote a letter to Biden in 2001. The senator responded in a handwritten note, saying, in part: "All that I can say is I am sorry for all of us and please know that neither I or my sons feel any animosity whatsoever."[176]

In the days and weeks after the crash, Joe wasn't sure if he would even be sworn into his Senate seat. His only concern was for his sons; he knew that he was their center, their only remaining parent, their closest connection to their missing mother and sister. "We can always get another senator," he said, "but they can't get another father."

He was persuaded to take it one step at a time, and so began his Amtrak commute. The second house that Joe and Neilia had been eyeing in Washington did not materialize, so Joe made the daily trek back home to spend time with his sons. He got a mobile phone in his car so they could reach him at any time.[177]

Biden took the oath to begin his Senate term in early January 1973, just eighteen days after losing his wife and baby daughter. He was sworn into office in the chapel of the Wilmington Medical Center with his sons nearby. Beau was in a bed, his leg still in traction; Hunter had been released already.[178] The ceremony was held with Joe's back to the national TV network cameras, so NBC reporter Peter Hackes persuaded him to do a do-over.[179] Joe spoke the words that thirty other Delaware men had sworn to before him before they started their terms for that seat:

> *I do solemnly swear (or affirm) that I will support and defend the Constitution of the United States against all enemies, foreign and domestic; that I will bear true faith and allegiance to the same; that I take this obligation freely, without any mental reservation or purpose of evasion; and that I will well and faithfully discharge the duties of the office on which I am about to enter. So help me God.*[180]

The men who had come before Biden to hold this Senate seat were prominent, powerful names in Delaware's heritage: Bayards and Claytons, Ridgleys and Comegys, Saulsburys and du Ponts. They represented the past. Now, a Biden, a young man from Scranton who had grown up in an apartment rather than a mansion, had joined their ranks. It was a time that was supposed to be a celebration, but it had transformed itself in a split second to a moment of personal and public sorrow. At that time, Joe was not even sure he would finish out the term, but he buckled down, cared for his kids and got the job done.

Later, New Castle County would name a park near Prices Corner Neilia Hunter Biden Park in Neilia's honor.[181] In New York, Cayuga Community College gives two Neilia Hunter Biden Awards for journalism and literature, and the Syracuse schools have a memorial to Neilia outside Bellevue Elementary School.[182]

A few months later, in March, Joe took to the stage at a Sussex County Democratic dinner, held at Wesley United Methodist Church in Georgetown, as the party's special speaker. He sat at a table rather than on stage with the rest of the elected officials and leapt to the lectern when it was his time, receiving two standing ovations.

He read his notes, jotted down on a napkin. "I very seldom have trouble speaking, as you know," he said in a mild joke. "But this is where we started."

His strong, powerful voice quivered. Joe began to cry. He pulled out his handkerchief and tried to keep going. "My wife had a great deal of respect for you all." He couldn't hold the tears back. "I didn't want to come tonight….I've never done this in public….I'm sorry." And he walked off the stage into the wings.

Officials rushed up to comfort him. The audience's tears, in sympathy with their senator, filled the church hall.

Two minutes later, Biden returned to the stage, offering stories from Capitol Hill and recounting his experiences as the youngest U.S. senator. He also spoke of Neilia's love and support and influence. And he tossed aside the trappings of his office, telling the Sussex audience that he was still just "Joe Biden, not Senator Biden."

"I'll try my best not to embarrass you," he said, and he received another standing round of applause.[183]

THE SENATE AND "AMTRAK JOE"

iden admitted at one point that his Senate performance was below his standards in his first term, when he was still in the early stages of grief. "I came to Washington with a helluva chip on my shoulder," he told the *New York Times* in 1987. "My first two years I was self-absorbed with my own problems."[184]

In his first week on the job, Biden stood at the doorstep of 517 Vandever Avenue in Wilmington alongside Mayor Tom Maloney, a friend since their youth, to announce his plan to turn abandoned city houses into homesteading sites.[185] It would have provided an estimated hundreds of thousands of empty houses for the purpose of homesteading across the nation; Wilmington alone had more than three hundred eligible properties. "We're now on a new frontier, a frontier right in the cities," Biden said.[186]

Biden would become known for numerous other domestic policy proposals that he put forward and passed into law. But what Biden would become known for most of all in the Senate—and a primary reason he became vice president—was his expertise in foreign affairs. He traveled far and wide, meeting players and cementing relationships that would pay off decades down the road, and he met many world leaders on trips to Washington, D.C. Former Senate majority leader George Mitchell of Maine recalled introducing heads of state around Capitol Hill. "I'd say, 'Here's Senator Smith, here's Senator Jones,'" Mitchell said. "When I got to Joe, the leader would look out and say, 'Hi, Joe.'" Biden's former national security advisor Julianne Smith remarked, "You can drop him into Kazakhstan or Bahrain,

Biden has developed globe-spanning relationships with world leaders. Here, he meets with Senator Frank Church and Egyptian president Anwar Sadat in March 1979. Sadat was assassinated in 1981. *Central Intelligence Agency.*

it doesn't matter—he's going to find some Joe Blow that he met thirty years ago who's now running the place....Over thirty-five-plus years, everyone came to the Senate Foreign Relations Committee."[187]

Each night, Joe would head home on Amtrak for that connection to his sons rather than stay in Washington to schmooze with lobbyists and reporters or strategize with his Senate colleagues. "He could kiss his boys goodnight and read them a book or be there for them in the morning to drop them off at school," Valerie recalled. "A lot of politicians espouse family values, but Joe lived them."[188]

Biden took advantage of the two-hour one-way commuting time and held meetings, interviews and strategy sessions while on board. Biden and Ted Kaufman shared the train for decades, shooting ideas back and forth, planning campaigns and forming nation-shaping policy. "We were back and forth on the train for 4,000,827 hours. So, we talked about everything," Kaufman remembered.[189] Biden also read *Architectural Digest* on some Amtrak rides, fuel for his real estate dreams.[190]

That ridership led to Biden's strong support for the national rail network. In 1981, he voted against Reagan's cuts to Amtrak, the only member of the Senate Budget Committee to do so. "You can't come back next year or the next year and change it," he said. "Those railroads will have gone."[191]

Built in 1908, the Wilmington Train Station was originally built for the Pennsylvania Railroad to replace a twenty-five-year-old building and was to be designed by architects Frank Furness and Allen Evans. The railroad required the new station to be put in beside the existing offices. Furness designed the station with the trains heading through the second floor so passengers could watch and listen to the trains as they pulled in and out. The clock tower was built using stone and terracotta.

The Wilmington Train Station is 1 of 18 surviving stations of the 180 Furness designed, and it earned him a $11,000 commission, one of his largest

Biden talks with reporters after a news conference in July 1994. Despite the workload, he never had a second home in the capital but commuted back and forth. *Library of Congress/ CQ/Roll Call.*

projects. Amtrak renovated the station in 1983 and again in 2009 in the face of rising ridership. An additional $11.6 million project was conducted by the Biden administration in 2023 to improve the station's accessibility and maintenance. Wilmington saw an annual ridership of 625,000 in 2023, with ticket sales reaching $50 million. The station now also serves SEPTA trains into Pennsylvania.[192] Wilmington ranks as the twentieth-busiest station in the United States.[193]

In 2011, the station was named in Biden's honor, capping a two-year renovation and refurbishment effort with a $37 million price tag. Biden said that seven more lanes would have to be built on I-95 if the train routes did not exist. "This is so critical, such a critical artery to the commerce and the intercourse of this great country, and quite frankly, this city," he said.[194]

The title of "Amtrak Joe" was bestowed by CNN during the 2008 campaign after Biden had taken an estimated eight thousand round trips on the Washington, D.C.–Delaware line. Biden announced his 1988 presidential campaign at the Wilmington Train Station, and Obama picked him up on Amtrak on the way to the inauguration. And in 2020, Biden whistle-stopped at several campaign locations around the country via train. Biden's

The Amtrak station in Wilmington was named after Biden in 2011. It is one of a handful of remaining stations that were designed by architect Frank Furness. *Dan Shortridge.*

infrastructure plan as president also prominently featured investments in Amtrak. "Imagine a world where you and your family can travel coast to coast without a single tank of gas, or in a high-speed train, close to as fast as you can go across the country in a plane," he gushed.[195]

He described the train as a community:

> *Amtrak wasn't just a way of getting home. It provided me, and I'm not joking, an entire other family. A community dedicated—professional and that who shared milestones in my life. And I've been allowed to share*

milestones in theirs. I've been to an awful lot of weddings and christenings, and unfortunately some burials as well. We're family.[196]

The mid-1970s were a tumultuous time, challenging for the young dad who was struggling to be a father and the young politician who was learning how to be a senator. At one point, Biden sat down with journalist Kitty Kelley for an interview in the *Washingtonian* magazine. What appeared in print under the title "Death and the All-American Boy" was a wreck, making Biden out to be "a man slightly unhinged," he wrote years later, still perturbed about his treatment in the article. It said his office had a photograph of Neilia's grave; it was in reality one of a series of historic photographs in Delaware of a cemetery in Old New Castle. The interview was "cut up" to portray Biden as "callow and brash," he said. As a result, Biden had to become more careful and close-mouthed with the press.[197]

In 1974, *TIME* magazine bestowed on both Biden and U.S. representative Pete du Pont the title of "Rising Leaders." The two were colleagues in the Congress, but some wondered if they would ever go head to head. "It was not too early to ask whether Delaware, which was in fact big enough for both of them, would be big enough for either of them," Cohen wrote. "Pete du Pont was Delaware royalty, Princeton and Harvard Law, the master of a Chateau Country estate that had a name and not a street number….Joe Biden was Sturm und Drang, storm and stress. He was the son of a car dealer, scratching his way up through Archmere Academy, the University of Delaware and Syracuse Law."[198]

In the early 1980s, one of Delaware's most powerful institutions was born: MBNA. The company was a credit card institution that eventually made up a large chunk of Delaware's economy. Its employees were also responsible for the largest bloc of donations to Biden's Senate campaigns at one point. The credit card sector in Delaware grew from then-governor Pete du Pont's single biggest legacy, the 1981 Financial Center Development Act, which opened the state's doors to the banking industry.

MBNA started as a spinoff from Maryland National Bank, which moved to Delaware in 1982 into a former A&P grocery store in Ogletown with five employees. By 1991, it was the first standalone credit card issuer on the New York Stock Exchange.[199] Biden was a supporter of MBNA's positions in the Senate. In 2020, Massachusetts senator Elizabeth Warren criticized him for working "on the side of the credit card companies." Biden also voted to deregulate Wall Street and the North American Free Trade Agreement, anathema to progressive activists today.[200]

Above: Credit card giant MBNA was started in a former grocery store in 1982. It was later located in this building on King Street in Wilmington. *Dan Shortridge.*

Left: Senator Biden and Governor Sherman Tribbitt in October 1973. The two won their seats the same year. *Delaware Public Archives.*

Biden became an icon in Delaware politics, but he never played the game as intensely as some of his colleagues. He could have taken control of the party infrastructure and leadership but declined to, instead putting forth the belief that a U.S. senator with time-consuming commitments in Washington, D.C., would not be able to execute on plans and programs as well as another.

What Biden did was "reorient its political compass," wrote Cohen, the chronicler of all things political. "Democratic statewide candidates no longer would be parochial or Dixiecrat in their thinking but aligned with the more progressive national party." In the words of the late James R. Soles, a professor of political science at the University of Delaware, "Biden made possible the beginning of a Democratic dynasty—not that it's going to win all the time, but that it will be a force to be reckoned with."[201]

8

JILL BIDEN

Jill Biden is a force to be reckoned with—a quiet influencer of her husband's politics and vision for years and a teacher at heart. Born in Willow Grove, Pennsylvania, she found her way south across the border to study English at the University of Delaware.[202]

Politics was not Jill's passion, but she cast her first vote in 1972 for the young Delaware councilman Biden in his ambitious campaign to take the Senate seat. She even stopped by his victory celebration at the Hotel DuPont that night. The chandeliers and marble dazzled her, to be sure, but so did the proud, happy Neilia Biden. The two shook hands and exchanged brief words—"Congratulations on your win," "Thank you so much"—and went on their ways through the party. "I thought about how picturesque their family was—the handsome young senator, trying to better the world; his beautiful, loving wife, representing their family, always there to cheer him on; and three adorable kids. Here they were, with the world at their feet, taking on the political establishment and winning."[203]

Jill's first marriage to the owner of a popular Newark bar ended in divorce. But in 1975, the year Jill graduated from the University of Delaware, Joe spotted her face on a poster promoting the New Castle County Parks that was hanging at the New Castle Airport, taken by photographer friend Tom Stiltz. She was twenty-three and gorgeous.[204] That March, Joe got her number from his brother Frank and gave her a call.[205] Jill broke another date to go to dinner and a movie with Joe, north across the Pennsylvania border, where fewer of his constituents roamed and could spot his face.[206]

Jill Biden, seen in 2009 in her role as Second Lady, is a teacher, author and advocate for servicemembers. She married Joe in 1977. *Library of Congress.*

They went on another date—and another and another. Their ties went deeper, and love grew. Eventually, an adoring Hunter, then six, and Beau, then seven, approached their dad: "We think we should marry Jill," Beau said, clarifying that by *we*, they meant Joe.[207] It wasn't for lack of trying; Joe had proposed to Jill four times and was rebuffed at each occasion, but she finally said yes.[208] Joe and Jill were married on June 17, 1977, by a Catholic priest at the United Nations chapel in New York City.[209]

The foursome quickly coalesced as a family, forged by loss and love, neither forgetting nor neglecting the past. Memories, both old and new, were important to cherish. Neilia was Mommy; Jill was Mom.[210]

Jill quickly took on the primary parent role, volunteering in the boys' school library or on the cafeteria line, making sure they got to Cub Scouts and their sporting events and preparing meals. "There were plenty of nights when it was just the three of them at dinner. I'd come home, and Jill would

The Wilmington airport has been the site of many Biden flights. As shown in this undated photograph, the airport was also where Joe first saw Jill's face on posters promoting county parks. *Delaware Public Archives.*

be laughing at the earnest help our two sons had been offering at running the house," Joe said. She was waylaid by the sheer volume of laundry that the boys generated; Beau earnestly put forward the idea that laundry should perhaps be a once-a-day chore rather than once-a-week.[211]

Despite being at Joe's side through six senate races and three presidential campaigns—and, finally, victory—Jill never gave up her career as a teacher, even after they moved into the White House.[212] She first taught at St. Mark's High School in Wilmington, a Catholic school that opened its doors in 1969.[213] Later, she became a reading specialist at Claymont High School and earned her master's in education in reading from West Chester University in 1981.[214] Jill also taught at the Rockford Center, a private mental health hospital, while simultaneously earning her master's in English from Villanova University.[215] The hospital opened in 1974 with sixty beds on Broom Street in Wilmington and is now much larger and located near Newark.[216]

In the early 1990s, Biden taught at Brandywine High School, which opened in 1958 and then took in the children of many DuPont innovators, engineers and chemists. "We were kind of in that pipeline where you were expected to go to college," one 1967 alum of the school recalled.[217] (Jill delivered her 2020 convention speech from her former classroom there, room 232.)[218] In 1993, Jill began teaching English at Delaware Technical Community College's Stanton campus, where she continued until Joe's election as vice president. She earned her doctor of education degree

Jill Biden taught English at Saint Mark's High School in Wilmington in 1976. *Delaware Public Archives.*

The Rockford Center, a Newark mental health facility, employed Jill Biden as an English teacher. *Dan Shortridge.*

Jill Biden also taught for many years at Delaware Technical Community College. She earned her doctor of education degree from the University of Delaware. *Dan Shortridge.*

in educational leadership from the University of Delaware in 2007. She continued teaching at Northern Virginia Community College, even while living at the Naval Observatory and the White House. [219]

On Inauguration Day 2021, Jill knew what she wanted to do first and went straight from the ceremony to record a message to the national guardsmen who had helped with the ceremonies. The day after, she did a Zoom call with eleven thousand teachers. She became a political force as well, visiting thirty-five states in the first year of Joe's term. She rarely talked politics—it wasn't her thing—but she was a communication channel between educators and activists and the White House, sharing insights with Joe.[220]

9

VICTORY REPEATED

Coming up quickly was Joe's first reelection campaign, the 1978 race. One afternoon, while on the Amtrak train from Washington to Wilmington, Joe and Ted Kaufman created a strategy for a hypothetical Republican who was aiming to end Biden's Senate career. The opponent focused their attacks on busing, civil rights, civil liberties and labeling Joe a liberal. "By the time we got off the train, Ted and I had convinced ourselves I could be beaten," Joe said.[221]

The Republican nominee in 1978 was James H. Baxter, a conservative Georgetown farmer—but in actuality, he was the more moderate candidate of the two Republicans in the primary, recalled Valerie Biden, who was serving a second round as Joe's campaign manager.[222] The campaign was fierce; at one stop at the Delmarva Chicken Festival on the Delaware State College campus in Dover, Biden was harassed by an angry woman about busing.[223]

But in the end, Biden beat Baxter by a 27,000-vote margin, 93,930 to 66,479. Delaware voters, at that time, were strong ticket-splitters. Biden won and a young man named Tom Carper was reelected as the state treasurer, but Republicans controlled the state's lone seat in Congress, as well as the attorney general and state auditor positions.[224] Biden held his election night victory bash at his alma mater Archmere Academy, which all three of his children would later attend. That evening, eight-year-old Hunter had his first glass of champagne.[225]

Biden in 1980, two years after winning his first reelection bid over Republican James Baxter. *Delaware Public Archives.*

As reporter Celia Cohen characterized it, "Baxter was down-home, and Biden was on his way to the big time." With the accident just six years in the past, it was still weighing heavily on the senator. "If I sat still, it just poured in on me. My escape was to travel. If I didn't exhaust myself, I was not in very good shape," Joe said.[226]

In the late 1970s, as President Jimmy Carter was struggling in the polls, a small group of Democratic consultants paid a quiet visit to Biden's home, known as The Station, including Bob Squier and John Marttila. Their pitch: Biden should challenge Carter in the primaries as a "compromise candidate." His youthfulness and energy would appeal to many voters. For Biden, it was a tough proposal. He had been an early supporter of Carter in his 1976 campaign. And besides, there was a lot to think about, including his real estate obligations. "I remember thinking: I have no business making a run for president," Biden recalled.

> *I was thirty-seven years old. I still had nights when I was brought up short by my life.*
>
> *I'd stop on the landing of the carved staircase at The Station and look out the back window at the two enormous wings off the back, and the size of the place just scared me. Holy God, I'd think, is this me? Have I made a mistake here? Am I flying too close to the sun? Tempting fate?*
>
> *And now we were talking about making a run at the White House?*[227]

Joe squashed the Biden White House talk that year, but it would not stop. In 1980, as he spoke to the Democratic National Convention in New York City, Delaware delegates hoisted a "Biden in '84" banner. In 1982, some, including pollster Pat Caddell, pushed him to challenge President Ronald Reagan's election bid, citing a need for a new generation of leadership and generational change. Biden turned them down in a Shermanesque statement: "If asked, I will refuse. If put on the ticket, I will refuse." (He still got one delegate's vote in the Democratic presidential nomination process in 1984; the delegate was a teacher from Maine.)[228]

Biden faced his own Senate reelection campaign in 1984, and Republicans had high hopes that it would be a tough contest. They pinned their dreams on Governor Pete du Pont, who had moved on from Congress to serve two terms in the top seat and turn the state's finances around in the process. A Republican poll in 1983 put Biden ahead of du Pont only slightly, 47 percent to 44 percent, with 9 percent of voters having not yet made up their minds. Reagan even put the pressure on du Pont with a White House invitation that July, much like Nixon had put pressure on Boggs to run more than a decade earlier. But du Pont said no thanks and retired from elected life for a few years.[229]

The Biden–du Pont rivalry dated to 1970, when the former was running for the county council and the latter for Congress. The two clashed at a candidates' forum over drugs and policing when du Pont declared, "We have someone here running for county council who really doesn't know what he's talking about."[230]

The governor instead put his support behind John Burris, a former state legislator and businessman from Milford, who stepped into the void. Burris was the founder of Kent/Sussex Tire Service and also the vice-president of Burris Logistics, a family-owned cold storage warehouse and transportation business. He was elected to the state's House of Representatives in 1976, the first Republican in two decades to represent the area. He was a minority leader in 1978 and a majority leader from 1979 to 1982.[231]

In October, the conservative First Baptist Church near New Castle invited thirty-four candidates to a Sunday event before the worship service. Burris got the most applause, but it was Biden's mastery of the moment that helped. He spoke, and spoke, and spoke—and he spoke from the heart. He explained his opposition to organized prayer in schools—a tough sell to this audience—by giving the sign of the cross and reciting a Catholic prayer. "How many of you want your children to pray that way?" Biden asked the Baptist congregation, who jerked back from the very thought of praying like a Catholic. With no one enforcing a time limit and daring to tell a U.S. senator that he had to stop, the result was a home turf filibuster that gave Burris only a short time to speak—and cut out the rest of the candidates from hoping for a chance.[232]

Burris tried manfully in the 1984 campaign, but he was no match for Biden, who took the race with 60 percent of the vote. That year saw Delaware's propensity for ticket-splitting, with Republicans taking the White

Biden and Governor Ruth Ann Minner at an event. Minner was the state's first female governor; she started out as a secretary to Governor Tribbitt. *Delaware Public Archives.*

House and governorship and Democrats winning the U.S. Senate, a single House seat, the lieutenant governor's job and the insurance commissioner's post.[233] Burris tried later, in 2000, to run for governor against Lieutenant Governor Ruth Ann Minner—a Milford vs. Milford matchup—but Minner won handily with 59 percent.[234]

Joe won reelection easily in 1990 over M. Jane Brady, a thirty-nine-year-old former deputy attorney general, with 63.6 percent of the vote.[235] Brady would go on to become attorney general, a state judge and a chairman of the Delaware Republican Party but got the boot from the latter role in 2023 in favor of an ultraconservative failed candidate for governor and attorney general.[236]

In 1996, Biden faced a challenge from Republican Ray Clatworthy, a U.S. Naval Academy graduate, marine pilot and prolific businessman.[237] Clatworthy fell well short that year; Biden won with 60 percent of the vote, or a sixty-thousand-vote margin, against the backdrop of the Clinton-Dole campaign.[238] Clatworthy would try again in 2002 but again came up empty, though he held Joe to 58 percent.[239] When Clatworthy died just before Christmas 2021, his obituary read: "As a patriot, he ran for United States Senate in Delaware twice against a gentleman for whose name we are at a loss."[240]

RETURN DAY

In the early days of Sussex County, election returns didn't happen instantaneously and appear on the television screen or radio waves. It took time to collect the ballots, convey them to the county seats and then count them, so residents used to "return" to Georgetown to hear the results as they were read. Return Day traces its history to the early 1800s, and while technology has sped up the process, that tradition has persisted. Return Day (not Returns Day or Return Days) is a uniquely Delaware event, taking place every two years the Thursday after Election Day. There is a parade, with election winners and losers typically riding in carriages together. High school bands compete for the crowd's attention, and an ox roast feeds the multitudes with free sandwiches.

The returns are read by a ceremonial town crier from the balcony of the county courthouse, which overlooks The Circle, the center of town. The Sussex County chairs of the political parties gather on stage to bury a hatchet in a box of sand to represent the burying of the hatchet and the disappearance of political enmity. (For a time, at least.)[241]

Return Day is an official holiday in Sussex County, giving kids a half-day off school to attend the festivities. The election results that are called out are just for Sussex, leading to some lopsided tallies and confusion in the audience, as Sussex has become more Republican while the state has become overwhelmingly Democratic. "Just us, southern Delaware, Sussex County, Georgetown," said former town crier Ronald F. Dodd. "It certainly got us together to be nice after something so divisive as an election."

Historian Thomas Scharf reported in 1888 that the event was largely a social one: "Often this crowd presents a motley appearance, some being dressed in costumes which were used in primitive times, and others purposely arraying themselves in an outlandish manner to give more zest to the spirit of the occasion." The event was canceled during World War II but returned in 1948, thanks to the work of businessman Nutter D. Marvel, who contributed his collection of carriages to convey the candidates along the parade route. It was also canceled during the COVID-19 pandemic in 2020.[242]

In 1972, Joe tried to skip Return Day, claiming he had bronchitis, but Boggs wouldn't let him off the hook. "I rode many times as a winner," Boggs said. "I'd be proud to ride with you."[243] At Return Day, Joe was emotional as he spoke about defeating Boggs, calling him "the outstanding senator from Delaware." Speaking to an estimated crowd of one thousand, Biden's eyes got watery, and Neilia cried openly. "I only hope I can come back here, win

After his Senate campaigns, Joe was a regular figure at the Return Day festivities in Georgetown. *Delaware Public Archives/*The Whale.

or lose, and have the respect from you that I have for this man," Biden said. "He's never done anything unethical or unfair in his life. He's displayed the moral character needed for the office." Boggs, for his part, spent a large part of the day thanking supporters and shaking hands. "I wish him all the success for the job," the senator said of Biden. "And I thank you for the honor and privilege of being with you."[244]

In 2000, Beau attended Return Day with Joe, which sparked talk about a challenge to Jane Brady for the attorney general position in 2002. Beau did not run then, holding his fire for 2006.[245] Joe returned to Delaware for a literal victory lap after the Obama-Biden ticket won the White House in 2008, riding with Jill in a horse-drawn carriage at the front of the parade, surrounded by Secret Service personnel and mounted law enforcement officers. His Senate opponent that year, Christine O'Donnell, rode in a separate carriage. "It feels great, it feels great," he said, waving to the cheering crowds who were standing in the rain to catch a glimpse. "This is home." The title of senator, Biden told the audience, "is the proudest title I've ever had."

"I may be the vice president–elect, but we're going to be home every weekend," Biden assured his fans.[246]

INSTITUTIONS AND ALLIES

Like Biden, Bill Roth was a Delaware institution for more than three decades. Originally from Montana, he came to Delaware by way of World War II and the Pacific theater, followed by an MBA and law degree from Harvard, funded by the G.I. Bill. In 1955, he was transferred to Delaware, where he became involved in community organizations and Republican politics. Roth ran for lieutenant governor in 1960 but lost narrowly, and he later served as a GOP state chairman. He ran for Congress and won in 1966, beating incumbent Democrat Harris B. McDowell Jr.

After two terms in the House, in 1970, with U.S. senator John Williams retiring, Roth ran for the Senate seat and won. Williams left office one day early, allowing Roth to have seniority over the other members of his Senate class. Roth was reelected four times, in 1976, 1982, 1988 and 1994.

Roth's interest was primarily in government finance and spending. In 1968, he created the precursor of the Catalog of Federal Domestic Assistance, a 1,034-page document listing assistance programs. He created the Roth IRA, spearheaded the Roth-Kemp tax cuts and exposed wasteful spending by the government.[247]

The 2000 campaign did not feature Joe on the ticket. But for Delaware observers, it featured a high-profile matchup between Roth for the Republicans and two-term governor and former congressman Tom Carper on the Democratic side. Delaware voters had largely bypassed any major political collisions between their top elected officials, but Carper was now upsetting the apple cart. The governor watched election returns that

Biden signs a photograph at the dedication for the Roth Bridge, which took place in the early 2000s after Roth's passing. *Delaware Public Archives*.

November with Joe and Jill at the Wyndham Garden Hotel, and Carper came out on top.[248]

Still, Joe confessed later, he could not bring himself to work against Bill Roth, a friend and colleague in the Senate for years. "Every year Bill Roth was up, I was out of state campaigning for other people," he said. Speaking to Roth at a post-election event, Biden said, "I don't think there was a single Biden that voted a straight ticket the last time you ran."[249]

Roth passed away several years after his losing reelection bid. The Roth Bridge, which spans the C&D Canal, was named in his honor.[250]

DOVER AIR FORCE BASE

One late-1970s Dover Air Force Base event was captured in photographs of Biden and Roth easily smiling and talking with military brass and each other. Delaware has just one major military base, and it serves as a central hub for cargo and servicemembers overseas. Dover Air Force Base began as a lowly municipal airfield, leased to the U.S. Army Air Corps in 1941.

Biden and fellow senator Bill Roth talk with a U.S. Air Force representative at a Dover Air Force Base event. *Delaware Public Archives.*

Later in World War II, it housed squadrons that ran antisubmarine sweeps; after new runways were built, Dover became a training center for fighter pilots flying the P-47 Thunderbolt. It also was home to a secret program that tested air-fired rockets. After the war, Dover adjusted to its new role ferrying troops and cargo under the Military Air Transport Services (later the Military Airlift Command).[251]

Dover now also supports humanitarian missions and serves as the entry point for the remains of all personnel killed in action around the globe. A large mortuary center on the base pays final respects to the fallen servicemembers, a tradition and a service that goes back decades. During the Vietnam War, a young Biden reflected on the impact of the base, both around the country and in Delaware: "Every week young American men were being shipped to the mortuary at Dover Air Force Base in body bags. How many mothers lay awake at night wondering how their own sons might return, and wondering what exactly they were risking their lives for?"[252] Dover also handled the remains of the astronauts who were aboard *Columbia* and *Challenger* and 9/11 victims. The current $30 million mortuary was opened in 2003.[253]

As the main mortuary for military servicemembers killed overseas, Dover has hosted Biden to pay tribute to the fallen several times in what is called

Biden has attended numerous dignified transfers at Dover Air Force Base over the years. This occasion, in 2021, honored sailor Maxton W. Soviak of Berlin Heights, Ohio. *U.S. Air Force.*

a dignified transfer. As National Public Radio describes it, "It is one of the most solemn tasks for a commander-in-chief, bearing witness as the bodies of fallen service members return to U.S. soil."[254]

TED KAUFMAN

Ted Kaufman got his start with Biden's team by taking a one-year leave from DuPont, where he was an engineer. He left twenty-two years later. In the meantime, he served as Biden's chief of staff, the senator's top aide, until retiring in 1994, and then he served as an advisor. He said his engineering background helped him and Biden approach problems. "I'm more left side of the brain—a scientist—and Joe Biden is more of the right side—a poet. That's what he used to say, and that was really true," Kaufman recalled.

When Joe moved into the vice presidency, his Senate seat in Delaware became open. Governor Ruth Ann Minner was able to appoint his replacement, and many theorized she would name Beau. But he declined, and she turned to Kaufman, Joe's former chief of staff. It was Hunter

Ted Kaufman was named to fill Biden's Senate seat until the next election could be held. Here, he is speaking at the 2010 Truman-Kennedy dinner in Bridgeville. *Courtesy of the Office of U.S. Senator Chris Coons.*

Biden's idea, floated on a flight from Chicago. In the end, Joe asked Ted, "Ruth Ann is going to call me. Do I tell her that you would be an excellent choice?" Ted said yes.

But Kaufman put a limit on his service. "The whole time I was in the Senate there were people who couldn't believe that I didn't want to run for reelection," he said. "It took them a while to figure out that I was serious. I wasn't going to run for reelection….I didn't want to serve beyond the two years."

As a senator, Kaufman got an uplifting of pride and praise from his old friends on the staff on both sides of the aisle and diligently pursued his passions and interests in representing Delaware. He was replaced by Chris Coons, the New Castle County executive. Coons was almost a sacrificial lamb. He was not supposed to win against the expected Republican hopeful, Congressman Mike Castle. But Castle was beaten in the primary by Christine O'Donnell, who later infamously declared in an advertisement: "I am not a witch." Coons defeated her handily, a beneficiary of the Delaware GOP's increasing slide into irrelevance.[255]

"Joe has long said that Ted Kaufman is the wisest man he's ever known. Ted is his true north, and Joe calls hiring Ted the best political decision he ever made," recalled Valerie.[256]

11

HOMES

At the start of 1971, even with bigger visions in his eye, Joe often loaded his family in the car and took them driving around in search of the home of their dreams. One day, he found it on North Star Road. It was about twenty minutes north of Wilmington, a 1723 Colonial-style home with impressively tall ceilings, built from stone with stucco overlaid. On four acres with a barn and pool, it was ready for the Bidens to move in. They put in an offer at the end of February and had loan papers drawn up in the first week of March. Joe called it the "House of Our Future."[257]

The problem was that North Star, as they would call the house, was outside of his council district, meaning if they moved, Joe would have to resign. The solution that Joe devised was elegant, if slightly inconvenient for his parents: Joe Sr. and Jean would move into North Star, and Joe and Neilia would move into their old house on Woods Road. He would stay in his district until he was free to move.[258]

The property on which North Star sits today once comprised three hundred acres of land. It was owned by T. Coleman du Pont, a president of DuPont and later a U.S. senator who held Biden's future seat. Now located on three acres, the home includes a den extension that Biden added. It has five fireplaces and a three-car garage.[259]

After a few years, the family recognized that North Star was not large enough to hold the family, so Joe went out driving and looking, as he was wont to do. He found a home on Montchanin Road in the community of Greenville, a grand house that had seen better times. Legend has it that

The Biden family settled into this house on North Star Road. Joe took out a $20,000 loan against it to keep radio advertisements on the air in 1972. *Dan Shortridge.*

he broke in through the plywood one night and fell in love.[260] The home had two wings that contained the bedrooms, a huge library, a ballroom, an expansive living room and a staircase "that Clark Gable could have carried a girl down," as a biographer described it. "Beautiful brickwork over the windows, black shutters, white porches, a fountain, a pool…the place is drop-dead stately."[261]

Joe bought the property for $185,000, about $1.1 million today, and sold the surrounding land to finance the remainder of the deal. He made $44,600 at the time. But the ten-thousand-square-foot mansion needed some work. A family of squirrels had taken up residence on the third floor, and there was asbestos in the basement. Joe and the kids went to work on weekends; the senator himself put on a full-body hazmat suit and tore the asbestos out on his own instead of paying a contractor. Father and sons planted hemlocks and yews and cypress trees all over the property.[262]

Before they were married, Jill saw the house in its early stages, prior to the contract's signing, and was somewhat dubious of the giant mansion. "Where I saw a grand house with children and grandchildren, she saw a leaky roof....She probably anticipated better than I did that I'd spend more on my heating bill the first year than on my mortgage payments," Joe said.[263]

Hunter recalled closing part of the house off in the winter to save on the heating bill and described the constant chore of painting: "Dad, Beau, and I painted one side of the house every summer; when I was younger, Dad dangled me by the ankles from the third-floor windows to slap paint under the eaves. By the time all four sides were finished, the front needed to be painted again and we started all over." The house ate Joe's cash for breakfast, in Cramer's words.[264]

But the work paid off, and the house was a comfortable, expansive and expensive home for many years. When Valerie Biden returned from her honeymoon—she had gotten married to Joe's Syracuse friend Jack Owens— she and her husband moved in to The Station along with Joe and the two boys. The home's crowded nature was why they dubbed it The Station, "for all the comings and goings," said Valerie.[265]

In the mid-1990s, with Beau and Hunter fully moved out and starting their own careers and lives, Joe and Jill sold The Station. They wanted to design their own house, to be built on property along Barley Mill Road. The buyer of The Station, MBNA vice-chairman John R. Cochran III, picked it up for the asking price of $1.2 million. [266]

Biden turned around and used the revenue from the sale to pay $350,000 in cash for 4.2 acres to developer Keith D. Stoltz, the same price Stoltz had paid a few years earlier. In 1997, he took out a $400,000 construction loan to build a new home and a pool. Joe, Jill and Ashley lived in rentals while their new home, which was later to be dubbed the Lake House, was being constructed.[267]

To be precise, the Lake House is located on a manmade pond, not a lake. But it represented the next move for the Biden family, and for Joe's "frustrated architect" passions. (Jill once suggested that she would pay for architecture school if he dropped out of the Senate.) At seven thousand square feet, the home was completely designed by Joe, and the family moved in in 1998. "If you went through, you probably saw all those significant number of house plans that I've drawn," he said.

Joe's especially proud of the library, with its rich wood walls, leather sofas and chandelier; the room cost one-third of the entire cost of the house. When he retired from the Senate, Joe bought the desk from his Capitol Hill office, as lawmakers are allowed to do. The garage holds Joe's golf clubs, tools and paint and Jill's pitchers, vases and crockery. To squeeze in his Corvette, Joe had to put their gardening and lawn equipment in a

Joe works the phone in his home office in Greenville in 2010. The newspaper on his desk carries a front-page story about Beau's health problems. *Barack Obama Presidential Library.*

storage center.[268] According to one reporter, Joe sometimes skinny-dipped in the pool. Jill would also bring her laundry back from Washington to do it at home.[269]

At the beginning of Joe's presidential term, the Secret Service oversaw a one-year security upgrade project, including improved fencing, barriers for vehicles and bulletproof windows. "I have no home to go to," he complained.[270]

One advisor said of Joe's travels home during his presidency: "It grounds him, to be honest, to go home and be in the house he built with Jill, with all the traditions, with his family nearby. That's what he loves. That's where he is rooted."[271]

12

ON THE TOWN

The Bidens have long been fans of Delaware's restaurant scene. Being out, about and seen is a good way to both connect with constituents and support local businesses, and if the food's not bad, that's a plus, too. The eateries they've dined at around the state could probably fill their own book, but what follows is a sampling of establishments in Wilmington that they enjoy.

Piane Grill, located on Market Street in Wilmington, was the location of Joe's thirtieth birthday party in 1971 that made him just barely old enough to serve in the Senate.[272] Piane (also called Pianni) was also the site of Wednesday night meetings of the Democratic Forum, a reform-minded movement with plans to change Democratic politics of which Biden was a part. He was the first member to win elected office.[273] Piane's was owned by Robert Piane, who ran multiple other restaurants in Wilmington and the country's first five-star catering operation.[274] In 1989, Biden was the speaker at an event for Piane Caterers' "Love Works" program, which makes donations to five city agencies for their food pantry programs. "His involving people has a ripple effect," Biden noted. "Hunger—and relieving hunger—crosses ethnic barriers and it crosses community barriers."[275]

Ristorante Attilio is an Italian eatery still operating on Lancaster Avenue. It was a favorite of Joe and Jill's and the place they chose for dinner after Joe ended his presidential campaign in 1987. People applauded when they walked in and rose to their feet. Run by the Perrino family, the restaurant has been around since 1985, and its fans are highly devoted.[276]

Mrs. Robino's Restaurant is a popular Italian dining establishment in Little Italy. Biden had lunch there with his sister, Valerie, in early 2024. The restaurant has been around since 1940 and is well-known for its large portions.[277]

Winkler's Restaurant, located at Fifteenth and French Streets in Wilmington, was where Rod Ward interviewed Biden for his first job as an attorney. It was operated by Harry and Nellie Winkler and their sons, Louis and Henry, until the mid-1970s. The eatery was founded in 1880 by Louis and Annie Winkler, operating out of the former carriage house and horse stables of the former Shipley Mansion. The Winklers demolished the mansion in 1957 in favor of a parking lot. Brothers Louis and Henry took it over in 1946, and in 1975, they leased it to a Maryland restaurateur. Winkler's closed suddenly in 1984 for renovations and never reopened. It later became the home of an advertising agency, whose employees were regaled with stories about New Year's dinners and marriage proposals by passersby.[278]

The Bidens have also supported many local stores and shops, particularly in Wilmington. Leonard Simon has selfies with Joe Biden, whose shirts he supplies from his shop on Wilmington's Market Street. But he won't show them to a soul. "The pictures are in my phone. That's where they will stay," said Simon, the owner of Wright & Simon. "I'm a small store in a small state. I have to have discretion." Simon's father, Morris Simon, helped cofound the

Winkler's Restaurant lasted from 1880 to 1984, based on the former stables and carriage house of the Shipley Mansion. *Delaware Public Archives.*

shop in 1935; it has been at its current location since 1952. Leonard Simon began working for his father in the 1960s, starting there full time in 1972. Today, a full custom suit can be purchased there for $795. Simon's clients want speed and service—no fuss, no muss. "They don't come here to chit-chat," he said. "They want to come in, order what they need, and get back to work."[279]

13

THE KIDS

The two elder Biden kids played and explored as all children did in the 1970s and 1980s. They built forts, walked along railroad tracks and rode BMX bikes on backroads. They bought hot dogs and snacks at convenience stores and gas stations, played video games and visited the local video store, called Gandalf's, to agonize over their tape of choice. They chucked acorns at cars along Buck Road ("horribly stupid and we freaking loved it," Hunter remembers) and played pickup basketball. Bored? Break out the BB guns.[280] There was no such label as "free range kids" back then—they were all roaming wild.

The Biden boys spent time at the Amtrak station, "where we were basically raised," as Hunter remembers. They also enjoyed digging in at the Charcoal Pit, a still-standing classic restaurant in northern Delaware. The Charcoal Pit was opened in 1956 on Concord Pike by brothers Lou, Samuel, Martin and Aaron Sloan, also founders of the Dog House in New Castle. The Charcoal Pit is known for its sandwiches and milkshakes and has been loved by teenagers in the way that hangout spots always are.

In the 1960s, the teenagers got so rowdy at the Pit after football games that management restricted the number of diners who could enter. High school students weren't allowed to hang out in the parking lot without a Pit burger and soda in hand. Especially popular were the high school–themed ice cream sundaes that matched the school colors. In 2014, President Obama swung by the Charcoal Pit to meet the customers and eat a cheeseburger, fries and shake—at Joe's recommendation. At the same

President Obama chats with a customer at the Charcoal Pit, a Biden family favorite, in 2014. *Barack Obama Presidential Library.*

time, Joe and Beau were dining at the Dog House. "I've spent so much of my adult life here. It's really affected me," said Lou Sloan, the last survivor of the Sloan brothers. The Charcoal Pit was sold to Louis Capano Jr. in 1986 and remains open and popular today. Hunter and Beau would order the black-and-white milkshakes (triple thick) and heaps of well-done fries to accompany their cheesesteaks.[281]

Born a year and one day apart, the boys alternated celebrations of their birthdays (February 3 and 4) and alternated their meals (spaghetti for Beau, chicken pot pie for Hunter) and desserts (vanilla cake with chocolate icing for Hunter, brownies for Beau).[282]

BEAU BIDEN

Beau's first memory, like Hunter's, was of the time after the accident. He also remembered the years of recovery—physical as well as emotional—and rebuilding a family with his father and brother before later reforging a family with Jill and Ashley. He recalled Joe jumping into bed with them for stories, holding and kissing them at night and, in the morning, dropping them at school on his way to catch the train.[283]

At age six, Beau was torn as only a child can be between his love for his newborn cousin Missy and his love for his late sister. "His conscience, forever near the surface, constantly troubled him," Valerie said. "That was Beau at six, and that was Beau for the rest of his life—caring, tender, loving, and kind, duty-bound, always holding himself to a higher standard."[284]

Beau had a high degree of personal responsibility and sensitivity to doing what was right. When Beau was around fifteen years old, he borrowed a 1960s Omega watch that was once Joe's gift from Neilia without asking but lost it at a dance. The guilt persisted. "He never told Dad, and Dad didn't even notice it was missing until long after. I'd forgotten all about it. But Beau remembered. He felt guilty about losing that watch forever," Hunter wrote later.

At Archmere, Beau was known as "the sheriff," the responsible one, the designated driver. "People knew that as long as their kids were with Beau, they were safe," Hunter recalls. Beau brought the hammer down on friends who were drinking too much and would tell them to stop—and they listened. He would wear the same clothes—khakis or jeans, a polo or button-down and loafers—and they were all lined up along the wall.[285] That responsibility and leadership must have been a heavy burden for a teenager to bear.

Beau was elected class president at Archmere, like his dad. Beau attended the University of Pennsylvania and went to law school at Syracuse, also like his dad.[286] He attended Penn during the time of Joe's presidential campaign,

Attorney General Beau Biden (*second from the left*) discusses servicemembers' financial issues during a roundtable at Dover Air Force Base in 2012. *U.S. Air Force.*

which just spread Beau's name across campus. At Penn, he was a diligent student but a bit of a prankster, one time hiding dead fish in his fraternity brothers' rooms.

"He was very, very modest and unassuming," remembered his retired history professor Bruce Kuklick. "Especially at a place like Penn, you get a lot of kids who are arrogant for many reasons. He had every reason to be arrogant, but he wasn't like that at all." His classmate Evan Haynes said, "Whatever silver spoon people perceived in his mouth frankly never existed. And he would have spit it out if it had."[287]

Beau did experience one particular challenge after law school, failing the difficult Delaware bar exam three times in the mid-1990s. The state's bar exam is widely regarded as being more difficult than others; at the time, it was offered just once a year and had a high required pass rate. Despite the early challenge, Beau went on to work for the U.S. Department of Justice in Washington, D.C., and as a prosecutor for the U.S. Attorney's Office in Philadelphia.[288]

In the early 2000s, he joined the Judge Advocate General's Corps in the Delaware National Guard, serving part time.

He also joined the firm that would become Bifferato, Gentilotti & Biden.[289] The thirteen-attorney firm included both Democrats, such as former U.S. attorney and former attorney general candidate Carl Schnee, and Republicans, such as GOP gubernatorial candidate and former judge William Swain Lee. Beau's fellow named partners, Vincent Bifferato Jr. and Ian Bifferato, were the sons of former superior court judge Vincent Bifferato Sr. These sons of powerful men were clearly cognizant of their legacy. Joe Biden was elected to the Senate at twenty-nine, and Vincent Bifferato Sr. was a judge at thirty. "As Beau points out, that makes us both over the hill," Connor Bifferato joked with a reporter.[290]

Beau married his close friend Hallie Olivere in 2002 in Nantucket, Massachusetts. Hallie attended the Tatnall School, graduating in 1991.[291] The two were runners; Beau often ran on Tatnall's campus, and Hallie's 5K times were reported in the local paper in the twenty-minute range.[292] In 2003, she and Beau bought a home on Greenhill Avenue in Wilmington, D.C.[293] After earning a master's of education degree in school counseling from Wilmington College in 1999, Hallie worked at Tatnall, hired in 2010 as an admissions counselor.[294] She was a Biden supporter early on, publicly signing a "Delaware Women Support Joe Biden" advertisement in 1996.[295] Beau was promoted to major in the national guard in 2011 in front of an audience that included his father. Hallie pinned his insignia on his uniform

Beau Biden, in his role as a captain with the Delaware Army National Guard, boards a plane headed to Iraq from Fort Bliss, Texas, in 2008. *U.S. Army.*

as the couple beamed a large, stifled grin at the other.[296] Today, Hallie is the chair of the board of directors of the Beau Biden Foundation for the Protection of Children and draws on Beau's legacy for inspiration.[297]

HUNTER BIDEN

Hunter was three when he lost his mother and sister, the core of his family. His first vivid memory is being next to Beau in his hospital bed, his older brother saying, "I love you," over and over. He has always been in the spotlight, his family always making national news.[298] "They were always together," Joe recalled. "From the time in the hospital after the accident when they were just little boys, to when Hunt helped with the strategy for Beau's first race for attorney general."[299]

The boys' younger sister Ashley says that you can't discuss Hunter without telling stories about Beau. "They were inseparable and shared a love that was unconditional," she said at Beau's memorial service years later. "There wasn't one decision where Hunter wasn't consulted first, not one day that passed where they didn't speak, and not one road traveled where they weren't each other's copilots. Hunter was Beau's confidant. His home."[300]

Hunter went back and forth between schools to find the right fit. He attended third grade at Wilmington Friends School; fourth and fifth grades at St. Edmond's Academy, an all-boys school; and was back at Wilmington Friends for sixth grade and onward.[301] He did his freshman year of high school at Wilmington Friends, while Beau was at Archmere, and then Hunter joined his older brother at their father's high school alma mater.[302] Hunter studied at Georgetown University and then attended law school at Yale.

He later married Kathleen Buhle, who was impressed by his look and air. "He carried himself with the elegance of a movie star," she said. Hunter and Kathleen were married in July 1993 in Chicago after an engagement party at Joe and Jill's house.[303]

While visiting Wilmington a few years later, Hunter interviewed for and was offered a job at Delaware banking powerhouse MBNA, which dominated the credit card sector in the state. Despite Hunter being offered a significant salary ("greater than anything I'd ever imagined someone our age earning," his wife said later), Kathleen was not joyful at the prospect. "A job at MBNA meant working in Delaware, and Delaware had never been part of our plan. We were supposed to be finding a way to move back to Chicago." Hunter

Hunter and Ashley Biden attend their father's presidential inauguration in January 2021. *Chairman of the Joint Chiefs of Staff.*

was hired on as an **MBNA** management consultant and later promoted to executive vice-president. The couple settled into Delaware, the only of their friend group who owned their home and had a baby, "giving us the feeling of being 'true grown-ups,'" Buhle remembered.[304]

The couple bought a house on Centre Road, a ten-thousand-square-foot home with six fireplaces and parts dating to before the Revolution—and spent time fixing it up. "Joe and I spent equal time at Home Depot, and we had a shared work ethic," Buhle remembers. In 1998, Hunter left MBNA to work in the U.S. Commerce Department under the Clinton administration. He left that role in 2001 to work as a lobbyist.[305]

But Hunter's family ties, his connections to Beau and Joe, were what pierced him to the core and gave him his center, even while battling his well-documented addiction. "Beau and Dad saw the best in me even when I wasn't at my best," he said. "Looking at them was like looking in a mirror and, instead of seeing an alcoholic or drug addict, seeing the healthiest me reflected back."

During the worst of Hunter's addictions, the family attempted an intervention. Joe, Jill, Hunter's daughters and two counselors were there at the Lake House. "I don't know what else to do," Joe said, in a confession of powerlessness. "I'm so scared. Tell me what to do."[306]

ASHLEY BIDEN

Born a decade after Beau and Hunter, Ashley Blazer Biden was the baby of the family who grew into her own in the public spotlight, though she sometimes shunned the exposure. Her brothers named her (with Jill's approval) and adored her with equal fervor.[307]

Ashley's memories of her father are of Joe being there, no matter what. "He was present every morning. I talked to him two days by phone, he was always home at night, most nights, to catch dinner and to tuck us into bed," she told an interviewer. "He had a rule that no matter where he was, no matter what he was doing, if us kids called, that was it. You got him out of the meeting."[308]

Ashley also partnered with her father's campaigns as a child. She participated in parades, door-knocking and other campaign events. But still, she says, her family kept things "super down-to-earth" and didn't make a big deal out of it. "I knew Dad took the train and was trying to solve the problems of the world. But as a little girl, he's just Dad," she recalled. "I would tell him he smelled like work because of the smell of his suit." She was recalled by her former sister-in-law Kathleen as "shy but sweet and polite, with a poise far beyond her twelve years."[309]

She attended Wilmington Friends School early on. Founded in 1748, the school originated as a place for educating Quakers and Black children who were denied public schools in the area. The building it first operated in comprised just twenty-four square feet, the original meetinghouse for the Wilmington area. The school grew especially rapidly after the Civil War, with its student population quadrupling. In 1937, it moved to its current location in Alapocas. The school has expanded multiple times and is, at the time of this writing, building a new lower-school complex. Only about 10 percent of the school's current student body identify as Quaker. Its alumni include Biden aide Louisa Terrell, Obama aide Dan Pfeiffer, writer and NPR host Linda Holmes, Delaware First Lady Tracey Quillen Carney (the daughter of Justice Quillen) and suffragist Mabel Vernon.

Many students at Friends had a special passion for creating change. "Their commitment to the environment and peace has made my kids become really well-rounded," one parent recounted. "The students there just have this ability to talk to people and engage with people." Ashley Biden's personal childhood cause centered on animals, organizing an anti-animal testing campaign in school and lobbying Congress to protect the dolphins that were often caught in tuna nets. Later, she decided to earn money by painting seashells and selling them as soap dishes. In high school, she attended Archmere, which had been transformed from an all-boys school to a coed institution in the 1990s. She was an athlete in school, playing lacrosse and field hockey.[310]

Ashley traces her time at Wilmington Friends to her early understanding of inequity and racism. "It was my mission to tackle structural violence and institutional racism," she said. "Why aren't people healing? Why are the most marginalized the most harmed, yet the least healed?" Perhaps inspired by that exposure and her father's campaigning, Ashley went into social work, working for a mental health clinic, a home for foster children, the State of Delaware's Children's Department and serving as the executive director of the Delaware Center for Justice. She earned her master's degree in social work from the University of Pennsylvania and her bachelor's degree from Tulane University. In 2023, she was applying for a doctoral program with the University of Pennsylvania, doing consulting work and working to start a trauma recovery center in Philadelphia.[311]

Both Hunter and Ashley Biden attended Wilmington Friends School, which was founded in 1748. *Dan Shortridge.*

Joe and his daughter Ashley watch a 2012 presidential debate in a hotel in Toledo, Ohio. *Barack Obama Presidential Library.*

People close to the Bidens said Ashley has always controlled her own voice, sometimes to the point of being "almost reclusive," in one person's words. She would seem to agree with that description, citing the state of politics today. "When I was growing up, kids were off limits, right?" she said. "You weren't allowed. It was kind of a mutual understanding that you just didn't really go after people's children....That's not what I signed up for."

"I finally feel like I'm in a place where I really know who I am, I know my worth," she said in 2022. "I know my family—who are honestly some of the most incredible, kind, compassionate humans, who have given up their life, really, for service to the American people."[312]

Despite Joe and Jill now living in the White House, Ashley talks to them several times a day. She calls Joe her best friend: "We talk all the time about everything from personal stuff to criminal justice. I think he trusts my judgment, and he's always there to be supportive and to listen and to learn."[313]

14

EYES ON THE PRIZE

Much has been written about the 1988 presidential campaign and what could have been. Some in Delaware didn't think it was possible that year. "It might be true that Biden is looking to the day he, himself, might be elected president, but I feel in my mind that he really feels he can't make it, not in 1988," wrote Bill Frank, a columnist for the *News Journal* papers.[314]

Still, the Bidens plunged forward, seizing the new generation theme in their teeth. A poster advertising the campaign kickoff—11:30 a.m., June 9, 1987—featured a family photograph. From left to right was a grinning Beau, a thick-haired Hunter, a tiny Ashley on her father's lap, Joe smiling wide with his shining teeth and Jill positioned as a voice of reason. The launch took place outside the Wilmington Train Station in front of a crowd of thousands, "in the way they once did when a political speech was a social event," Cohen said. A banner hung overhead read, "YOUR FUTURE NEEDS JOE BIDEN."[315] After the speeches, a high school band played "It's a Small World After All" as the train pulled out; on board were Joe Sr. and Jean; Joe's brothers, Jimmy and Frank, and his sister, Valerie; Joe; Jill; the kids; and even more Bidens. (Of special note was Biden's revitalized hairline. He told a reporter who inquired about whether he'd gotten hair transplants, "I've got to keep some mystery in my life.")

The campaign began with $2 million in the bank and hopes for more. But it went south due to charges of plagiarism and questions about Biden's integrity. There were a few high moments, but the pressure of the campaign, combined with the Robert Bork hearings, was tough, leading to a siege

Biden outside the Wilmington train station in 1987 at his presidential campaign kickoff. The banners read: "Your Future Needs Joe Biden" and "Biden for President." *Delaware Public Archives.*

mentality at the Biden house. Reporters hung out nearby, and helicopters flew above. "The Station had become the Alamo," Biden said. Eventually, Joe dropped out; the campaign was a distraction from the important work of choosing a new supreme court justice. It was September 1987. The Biden campaign had lasted just four months. But Joe was forty-four years old, and there would be other campaigns.[316]

After Joe dropped out, he and Jill went to one of their favorite Wilmington eateries, Ristorante Attilio's, where they were quasi-regulars. "Our presence was never a big deal, but I worried that this night would be different," Joe remembered. The full dining room began murmuring when the coupled walked in, and then it got louder and louder. "All of a sudden one guy in the dining room started clapping," Joe said. "Then there was a smattering, and then it seemed like everybody at Attilio's was on their feet, giving me a standing ovation."[317]

That election cycle saw two Delawareans enter, Biden and former governor Pete du Pont, who similarly failed to catch fire. When du Pont pulled out after the New Hampshire primary, Cohen concluded that he had taken "the last of the glorious fantasy of a Delawarean in the White House with him when he went. It had always seemed too good to be true, and it was."[318] Little did any of us know how wrong that prediction would turn out to be.

During this time, Biden was plagued by headaches. When they became overpowering, he realized something was wrong. He made his way home from a trip in a haze of pain and asked his staff to help him to his bed.

Saint Francis Hospital in Wilmington first treated Biden for his aneurysm in 1988. He was quickly taken to Walter Reed in a snowstorm. *Delaware Public Archives.*

"They barely got me upstairs to my bed and then watched in horror as I curled up again into a fetal ball," he remembered.[319] Joe found himself at Wilmington's Saint Francis Hospital in a snowstorm. "The Bidens have spent an inordinate amount of time in that hospital," Valerie said. By the time she was able to make it to Saint Francis, Joe was already going out the door to Walter Reed, aboard a gurney that was en route to the ambulance.[320] He had been diagnosed with a brain aneurysm and underwent two critical surgeries at Walter Reed in February and May. Hunter, then eighteen, visited him nearly every weekend. The left side of Joe's face was drooping from nerve damage, his head was shaved, and staples made their way across his bare skull.[321]

At the Democratic National Convention in July, which nominated Massachusetts governor Michael Dukakis, the still-recuperating Biden got two votes from New Castle County party chairman Gene Reed and county treasurer Bette Rash.[322] It took months for him to get out of the hospital and recover.

He returned to public life in late August at the Sussex County Democratic Beach Jamboree before an audience of seven hundred.[323] The event is a unifying get-together that focuses the attention on the Republicans at the start of the fall campaign and coalesces Democratic energy around the candidates.[324] Friends and supporters swarmed Joe at Cape Henlopen State Park, near Lewes, touching his clothes and hands and hugging him.[325] "The good news is that I can do anything I did before," he quipped. "The bad news is that I can't do anything better." Two days after Labor Day, Biden reboarded Amtrak for his return to Capitol Hill, and he was greeted with balloons and signs of encouragement from the railroad staff. Biden was back.[326]

Some say that if Joe had continued his campaign and not dropped out when he did, he would have died. That's what Kaufman believes. The headaches wouldn't have halted him; he would have continued campaigning, and the aneurysm would have killed him. "He was unlucky in the confluence of events that ended his campaign, but he was lucky that he was not in the campaign the following February when he went to the doctor with a headache and, through emergency surgery, avoided dying from a brain aneurysm," Kaufman said.[327]

15

PROFESSOR BIDEN AND BEAU'S RISE

In 1991, Biden began a seventeen-year stretch of teaching a seminar on constitutional law at Widener Law School, now Delaware Law School, which lasted until he joined the Obama ticket. He taught some courses solo, while joining forces with Professor Bob Hayman for others. The course format, "Selected Topics in Constitutional Law," gave Biden the flexibility and freedom to share spur-of-the moment insights and observations from Capitol Hill. The classes sat around a table to facilitate discussions and observations. The course had a wait list for each of the seventeen years Biden was there. "He's very interested in the students, and he will stay and chat with them after class and just keep going and going," said the assistant dean for records and registration.

"He wanted an involved interactive discussion with everybody," said Joanne Spruill, class of 2008. "He would say things like, 'Colin Powell called me today,' and we would all be star struck that he would have those interactions, but because he was so down-to-earth in the class, you almost forgot who he was as a senator at the time."

Student Rob Sobol echoed Spruill's description. "He comes in and takes a call from the secretary of state at 8:30 in the morning, and two hours after class he has to catch a flight to Moscow to meet with Yeltsin," Sobol said. "He's a very demanding professor, and even if he were not a U.S. Senator, he would be one of the best professors I've ever had."

One law student, Claire DeMatteis, joined Biden's staff after graduation. She went on to serve as both the Delaware secretary of correction and

Joe taught a constitutional law seminar in the main law building at Widener University's Concord Pike campus for many years. *Courtesy of Delaware Law School.*

secretary of human resources under Governor John Carney (himself a onetime Biden staffer).

One class trip to watch a Senate committee meeting stuck with Spruill. Biden spoke with them about the importance of equality and the need for public service. "I wanted to be president…but this is bigger than me. This is historic," Biden told them.

"I thoroughly enjoy teaching at Widener and sharing my experiences with students," Biden told a university writer in the late 1990s. "It's a lot of work preparing for each class and grading papers, but it's something I believe in."[328]

Talking, telling stories and sharing anecdotes is how Joe connects with people and builds relationships. But it can also turn some off, as his friends have noted. ("Shoot. Me. Now," his colleague Barack Obama once scribbled on a note to an advisor while Biden held the floor at a hearing.)[329] At times, journalists have noted it is almost like a compulsion.[330]

Once, journalist and *Black Hawk Down* author Mark Bowden took a train ride into Wilmington while sitting across from Biden at a table; the senator talked "animatedly for the entire seventy-minute trip," Bowden said. "When he stopped off at Wilmington Station, the sudden silence in the car seemed like a physical presence, the onset of a vacuum. When I described the

Biden speaks at Downs Lecture Hall on the Delaware Tech campus in this undated photograph. *Delaware Public Archives.*

experience to a friend who'd taken the same ride more than once, he nodded knowingly and said, 'We call it getting "Bidened."'[331]

In 2004, Biden was ranked as the "top talker" in the country by *Roll Call* for appearing on more Sunday morning news talk shows than other member of Congress.[332] Yet despite his reputation as a voluble chatterer, Biden doesn't leak secrets or share confidential information—he just talks, full of openness and friendship. "What you see is what you get, and what you get is what you see," a senior aide once said.[333]

For Biden, it goes beyond merely blaring information in a one-way talkfest; he delves into deeper conversations, especially with his students. "I can't book anything in that classroom after his class because he stays so long to speak with students," recalled Dorothy Hemphill, assistant dean at Widener Law School.[334]

In the fall of 2002, Joe's father, Joe Sr., died at the age of eighty-six, at Joe and Jill's home. Politics was not Joe Sr.'s passion, but he was proud of his son and family. He had worked in many fields, doing what it took to keep his home and health together. He had been a sales rep for an oil company in Pennsylvania, an executive of a water sealant company during World

War II, the owner of an airport and crop-duster company and a car and condo salesman. Born in Baltimore, he lived in Wilmington and Scranton as a child, graduating from Scranton's St. Thomas Academy. His obituary echoes a sentiment often expressed by Joe Jr.: "He valued his reputation as an honorable man and as a family man, and with his wife he conveyed his values consistently to his children and their children. Both at home and in the business world, his word was his bond and he was proud of that."[335]

In 2006, Beau formally entered his father's field and ran to become attorney general of Delaware. It was his first run for elected office, and it was a powerful one at that—the state's top law enforcement officer and head of the Department of Justice. But the year was a good one; Joe was not on the ballot, so critics couldn't overtly claim he was trying to run on his father's coattails.

That year, Valerie's daughter, Missy, teamed up with Beau to run his campaign. "They were two cousins who grew up together in each other's homes, in campaign headquarters, at rallies, speeches, parades, and debates; they grew up often in the glare of harsh lights, but always with the security of family. They were two cousins holding one baton," Valerie proudly recalled.[336]

Beau ran against Ferris Wharton, a longtime state prosecutor and chief deputy attorney general for the state. Wharton had led the felony trial unit,

Biden chats with a reporter from a Dover radio station at an arts festival in this undated photograph. *Delaware Public Archives.*

Left: The Carvel State building, named for former Governor Elbert Carvel, was the headquarters of the Delaware Department of Justice led by Beau Biden. *Dan Shortridge.*

Below: Governor Jack Markell and Attorney General Beau Biden speak about new open government measures in 2011. Beau once planned to run for governor but was stricken by brain cancer. *Delaware State Senate.*

Beau Biden speaks at the 2012 Delaware State Police Memorial Service to honor troopers killed in the line of duty, held at Saint Polycarp Catholic Church in Smyrna. *Office of Governor Jack Markell.*

drug unit and rape response unit and had also been the lead prosecutor for both Kent and New Castle Counties. After leaving the Department of Justice, he worked as an assistant U.S. attorney. (After losing to Beau Biden, he worked as an assistant public defender and was then appointed a superior court judge.)[337]

The results were a mixed bag for both parties, as Democrat Tom Carper was reelected to the Senate, Republican Mike Castle kept his House seat, and Beau swung the attorney general's office back into the Democratic column with 52.6 percent of the vote.[338] He was sworn in on his family's 1893 Bible.[339]

Beau took over a large state agency, responsible for both civil litigation on behalf of the state and criminal prosecutions. Unlike other states, Delaware has no county-level district attorneys, only the state attorney general's office. As head of the Delaware Department of Justice, Beau primarily worked out of the Carvel State building in Wilmington. Built in 1977, it is the state government hub in New Castle County; the governor and many other agencies also have offices there, and more than one thousand people enter it every day. The building is named after former governor Elbert Carvel of Laurel, one of the men who persuaded Joe to consider running for the Senate in 1972.[340]

Over the years, Beau oversaw two tough cases in particular, the prosecution of a man who shot and killed a Georgetown police officer after a chase and the investigation and prosecution into a Lewes-area pediatrician who recorded videos of himself abusing and molesting eighty-five young patients.[341] He cited the latter case as one reason not to run for Joe's Senate seat when his father left to become vice president. Protecting children was a key plank of his platform while running in 2006, and he created an anti–child predator unit in the Department of Justice. Protecting kids, said friend Margaret Aitken, "was an enormously important part of his mission and what he wanted to do. I think that was born from a really honorable, honest place in him as a dad."[342]

16

THE VICE PRESIDENCY

The Biden family had been talking about a second White House run for Joe for years. As far back as 2004, Jill called a family meeting just before Christmas to discuss the 2008 campaign. The meeting involved Beau, Hunter, Ashley, Valerie and Ted Kaufman. "I want you to run," Jill told him forcefully. "We think you can unite the country." It took some time, but in 2007, Joe announced his campaign on *Meet the Press*. He told the host and audience, "I'm going to be Joe Biden, and I'm going to try to be the best Biden I can be. If I can, I got a shot. If I can't, I lose."[343] As we know from the benefit of hindsight, voters didn't agree. A Democratic campaign with the prospect of the first woman president and the first Black president didn't attract much attention for a Biden, no matter how good his campaign was, and Biden dropped out after the Iowa caucus results.

But the journey wasn't over for Joe. He had impressed Barack Obama, the eventual nominee, and the two talked that June about Joe joining the ticket as vice president. Joe refused. "I'll help you any way I can, but I don't want to be vice president," he told Obama. Obama insisted that Joe talk with his family before turning down the offer, and the family met in Joe's study. It turned out that they all wanted Joe to take the second-place slot; Jill, Beau, Hunter and Ashley were all in agreement.[344]

First, he had to pass the vetting process. Joe held a secret meeting with Obama's advisors David Axelrod and David Plouffe across the border at Valerie's house in Pennsylvania after flying in to the New Castle Airport. Biden ruled the conversation from the start, launching into a twenty-minute spiel. "Ax and I couldn't get a word in edgewise," recalled Plouffe. (Plouffe is himself a graduate of the University of Delaware and St. Mark's High School, where Jill once taught.)[345]

The financial vetting was simple: the Bidens owned no stocks. They had Joe's Senate pension, Jill's teacher pension, some certificates of deposit from Jill's mother and their home equity. "This all there is?" Obama asked. "That was one of the easiest vets in the world. You own nothing." (Joe was, in fact, elected while six figures in debt, including the mortgage on their new house, cosigning on their children's student loans and other loans.)[346]

One night, when Joe was known to be on the short list, Jill persuaded Joe to get away from the chaos. So, they slid out the back door, cut through the neighbor's lawn and were picked up by Beau. The two walked around in the dark to get some peace and quiet. Joe got the call that he was selected while in the waiting room at the family's dentist; Jill was undergoing a root canal after her classes that day. Biden himself told Obama that he needn't be concerned with endorsing his vice president or anyone else as a successor.[347]

The morning of Biden's announcement as the vice presidential pick, Jean Finnegan Biden waved farewell to the rest of her family as she headed off for an event with the Obama clan. She later attended the Democratic

Biden speaks at the 2008 Democratic National Convention, where he and Barack Obama were nominated for the nation's highest offices. *Library of Congress.*

National Convention, which was held in Denver, joined the family at Chicago's Grant Park on election night and loved seeing her son become inaugurated in January.[348]

The rest of the campaign season seems like a blur looking back. The Sunday before the convention, Joe attended mass at St. Joseph's and sat in the pews near the back to avoid disturbing any other churchgoers. When his presence was acknowledged by Reverend Joseph Rebman, his eyes went down to his lap, and he made the sign of the cross when prayers were requested in his name.[349]

Two days before his debate with Republican vice presidential nominee Sarah Palin, Biden returned to familiar surroundings in Delaware. He greeted Gert Boyle, who had been a fixture since Joe was at Archmere, at the cash register at the Charcoal Pit before sitting down to lunch with Beau, his wife, Hallie, and their daughter, Natalie. Joe had a cheesesteak and a black-and-white milkshake. Banners were going up around the state: "Delaware's Joe Biden." He may have been born in Scranton, but Delaware had supported him and now claimed him.[350]

Joe began Election Day at the Tatnall School, close to his home on Barley Mill Road, to cast his vote. He arrived shortly after 9:00 a.m. with Jill, Ashley and his mom, Jean. People waved "Delaware For Biden" signs outside the school. "Don't tell them who you voted for now," he joked to his mother. He then boarded a plane and flew to Virginia and Chicago for the final campaign stops.[351] On the stage on election night in Grant Park, after enough votes were in, the Obamas and Bidens stepped onto the stage to the roar of the crowd. It was a historic night. The Bidens had arranged for Beau, with his unit, to be there from Baghdad via Skype to celebrate, carrying a laptop onto the stage. "I felt a surge of pride," Jill recalled. "When we walked out on the stage to a roar of a million voices, we turned the laptop so Beau could see the crowd. In that moment, my family was together again."[352] Joe was as close to the White House as anyone thought he would ever be, the first Delawarean to rise so high.

To head to Washington, D.C., for the inauguration, the Obamas and Bidens joined forces via train. Obama picked up Joe en route to the capital via a special Amtrak train, recalling his vice president's many trips on the same route over his years of public service. Conductor Gregg Weaver introduced Joe as "Amtrak's no. 1 commuter," and Joe confided to the cheering crowd that when he was running late, he'd sometimes call ahead and ask them to hold the train: "There was always some mechanical difficulty that prevented it from leaving."

Joe and Jill Biden join Barack and Michelle Obama at the 2009 inaugural parade from the reviewing stand in front of the White House. *Library of Congress.*

Standing at the Wilmington Train Station, Obama recalled the history, heritage and legacy of freedom that had sprung from this small state. "It was here, in Delaware, that the Constitution was first ratified. It was here, in Delaware, where the First State joined our nation," the president-elect said. "Now it falls to us to carry forward that American story, and to make it our own."

In Washington, the inaugural parade included four Delaware marching bands from Delaware State University, the University of Delaware, the Delaware Volunteer Firemen's Association and A.I. du Pont High School.[353]

So, after thirty-six years, Joe gave up the Washington, D.C.–Delaware train ride for a much shorter commute in service of his president. The Bidens moved into the Naval Observatory, the official resident of the vice president, just several minutes from the White House. The change allowed him to continue attending his grandchildren's events at their schools and to have breakfast and dinner with Jill and his family. There were some other perks of the job, too. With Beau's unit in Iraq for the Fourth of July, Joe visited him and the troops overseas. He greeted his son upon his return to Delaware in the fall with a welcome home event in Dover.[354]

Joe knew going into the Obama administration that he had a special role. Despite the oft-used label of the Obama-Biden administration, he was second fiddle to a fellow charismatic, dynamic politician. Obama represented the same generational change that Joe once had. He was still leading but was doing so behind the man in the Oval Office, providing advice rather than making the final decisions.

Three days before the end of the Obama administration, Joe and Jill welcomed the Delaware National Guard home at the Chase Center on the Riverfront. *U.S. Air National Guard.*

It was a fundamental change after decades in the Senate. "I have never in my entire life had a boss," Joe recalled years later at a forum with former vice president Walter Mondale. "You get asked your opinion as a senator and my whole life I'd say, 'This is what I think.'" But Biden was no newbie to the job. He brought the most impressive resume and the longest service compared to any other vice president in history, including former speaker of the house John Nance Garner, the vice president to Franklin Delano Roosevelt, and Lyndon Baines Johnson, the second to John F. Kennedy.[355]

Joe was a caring boss to his White House staff. He once sent out a memo that said, "If I find out that you are working with me while missing important family responsibilities, it will disappoint me greatly." Family was always first with the Bidens, no matter what else was happening. In one photograph by White House photographer David Lienemann, Joe and Beau can be seen in a Dover office before a police memorial service. Joe is seated at a desk; Beau, his firstborn son and political heir who was then running for reelection as attorney general, is leafing through a book. It is a reminder of the closeness between father and son and the shorthand language they shared.[356]

The challenges of running the country were significant, but there were some celebratory moments. During Joe's first campaign for the Senate, he

The official vice presidential portrait of Joe Biden, which was taken in 2013 in his West Wing office. He was one of the most influential vice presidents in history. *Library of Congress.*

consulted with a Kennedy staffer named Paul Kirk, asking him for advice from the Kennedy experience. Kirk told him of the neighborhood teas that the Bidens adapted into coffees. In 2010, after the passing of Senator Ted Kennedy, Biden swore in Paul Kirk as the new U.S. senator from Massachusetts for the remainder of the term.[357]

President Obama and Vice President Biden speak to a crowd of 2,200 soldiers from the 101st Airborne at Fort Campbell, Kentucky, in 2011. *U.S. Army.*

There were also pleasant family moments. Ashley graduated with her master's degree in social work from the University of Pennsylvania in 2010, the same year she was introduced to her future husband, Dr. Howard Krein, by Beau and Hunter.[358] The couple was married two years later, their June reception held in the Bidens' backyard. White House photographs documented the celebration, with Joe hugging Jill tight during preparation time and Joe dancing the hora with Ashley.[359] Later that year, Beau, who was on the ballot rather formally as "Joseph R. Biden III," won reelection to a second term as attorney general. The Republicans had not bothered to nominate an opponent, so a minor party candidate was his only challenger; Beau walked away with 78.9 percent of the vote.[360]

These years also came with losses. At the age of ninety-two, Biden's proud mother, Catherine Eugenia "Jean" Finnegan Biden, passed away in early January. She was small, standing just five feet, one inch tall, but she was strong and tough. She was a rock for her family, blunt but full of wise counsel. "She was somebody I could talk to about anything and get good advice," said then-senator Ted Kaufman. "She was the kind of person who was always giving good insight into where you were coming from and could tell when you were upset about something and could pick you up." Joe recalled at the 2008 Democratic National Convention, "When I got knocked down by guys

Biden steps into a voting booth for the 2010 primary at the Tatnall School, which several of his grandchildren have attended. It's less than a mile from Biden's home. *Barack Obama Presidential Library.*

Announcing the First State National Monument in 2013 were (*from left to right*) Interior Secretary Ken Salazar, Vice President Biden, New Castle mayor Don Reese and Senator Tom Carper. *Office of U.S. Senator Chris Coons.*

Fresh off a reelection triumph, the Obama and Biden families take the stage in Chicago in 2012. The Democrats won Delaware that year with 58 percent of the vote. *Barack Obama Presidential Library.*

bigger than me, she sent me back out and demanded that I bloody their nose so I could walk down that street the next day." Jean Biden, who was sitting in the audience, mouthed "That's true."[361]

Biden also got to spend some time in Delaware as the vice president. He delivered the University of Delaware's commencement address in 2014, though he skipped the cap. (One Biden rule is to not wear funny hats.) He was greeted with thunderous cheers from four thousand University of Delaware graduates in blue robes, honoring their fellow alumnus. The provost, who introduced Joe, slipped up and called him "the forty-seventh president of the United States." The audience reacted with gasps and laughter, but no one—not even Joe—corrected the record.[362]

At the Democratic National Convention in Charlotte, North Carolina, held in 2012, the Democrats geared up to take on the Republican ticket of Mitt Romney and Paul Ryan. Beau adjusted Joe's tie in the wings before Jill headed on stage for her moment. Obama and Biden slid into victory, taking 51.06 percent of the vote over the Romney-Ryan ticket. In Delaware, the Democrats won with 58.6 percent.[363]

17

BEAU'S DEATH

B eau's first stroke, in 2010, was felt by Hunter, who woke early that day and experienced a world out of sync. "There was always this connection between the brothers that seemed beyond the physical," Kathleen Buhle recalled. Beau recovered, but it was ultimately only temporary. In August 2013, he experienced a grand mal seizure after an eleven-hour car ride from Delaware to Michigan City, Indiana, for a vacation.[364] That was the beginning of a painful time for Beau and his family, especially his brother and father, who remembered their previous losses that they still felt and could not bear to feel again.

For Joe, Beau was a son, a friend and an advisor, the only other member of the family who had held the burden of elected office. Hunter looked out for his brother during his treatments and tests, while Joe was regularly on the phone, calling to check in. "My answers were almost always the same: yes, and no," Hunter recalled. "He read into those responses what he needed to: in choppy times like these, he, Beau, and I could communicate through a kind of nonverbal frequency we'd developed during previous setbacks and injuries. Saying much more risked breaking the spell and going to a place none of us wanted to go."[365]

Beau underwent radiation, surgeries and a final direct injection of an experimental treatment into the tumor that was lodged in his brain. None of it worked. He grew weaker and weaker. He stepped down from the attorney general's office in 2015, ostensibly to focus on a campaign for the governorship in 2016. His physicians said he should if he wanted to: "Run for governor. Have a purpose," one told him.[366]

In April, the Bidens gathered in Joe's home library for a special event that excited countless 1980s kids, a special taping of *Reading Rainbow* with actor and host LeVar Burton. Jill and Joe sat on opposite sides of the couch, with their grandchildren Natalie and Hunter between them. They read from Jill's new children's book *Don't Forget, God Bless Our Troops*, which was fundamentally about how the kids dealt with Beau's long absence in a dangerous place. They laughed with Burton while telling stories.[367]

The books that sat behind them on Biden's shelves included many about politics, global affairs and conflict: *The Price of Power: Kissinger in the Nixon White House*, by Seymour M. Hersh; *To End a War*, by diplomat Richard Holbrooke; and the *Catechism of the Catholic Church*. Peeking over Joe's left shoulder were copies of his autobiography, published in 2007, and a biography of himself by journalist Jules Witcover.[368]

Beau was there, but he was in the background. He sat in the sunroom as the kids joked with Burton. With the windows open, he could feel the warm breeze from the lake. "This was his favorite spot in the house," Joe recalled. "Jill always said we were going to will our property to Beau, he loved it so much. We could find ways to even things out for Hunt and Ashley, she said, but Beau should have the house."[369]

That was not to happen. The sheriff could fight no longer. Beau returned to Walter Reed and was taken off life support on May 29, 2015. He died a day later, at 7:51 p.m. "It happened," Joe wrote. "My God, my God. My beautiful boy."[370]

Beau Biden's death crushed Delaware, almost as much as it flattened the Bidens. "He was a very decent person. He just did the right thing," said Bill Quillen, who had advised Joe on careers decades earlier. "That was the governing principle of everything he did. I mean, he didn't have to serve in the National Guard." He noted that Beau had much more to give the state: "Joe was a big shadow. Beau was never fully appreciated for what he was."

"He was a gentleman, a man of deep-seated belief that above all, the highest calling was as a public servant," said Lisa Goodman, the president of Equality Delaware. Tim P. Mullaney Sr., who was the Department of Justice chief of staff under Beau, said he had expected Beau to make a full recovery: "I thought he was going to be fine. I just felt that Beau was going to be there. He just had this spirit."[371]

"He was just innately kind. He had a complete aversion to ever hurting anyone's feelings," recalled Terry Wright, a former Joe Biden aide who had known Beau since 1982.

Developer Rob Buccini remembered a day when the two were driving home from college. Near Scranton, Biden was pulled over for speeding. The police officer saw his name and wanted to just give Beau a warning, but that was a nonstarter. "He made the police officer give him a ticket," Buccini said. "He never acted with an air of entitlement. Because of who he was, he worked harder to be humble."

To Beau, family was first, many friends remarked. "Beau never wanted to be anything other than Joe Biden's son," recalled attorney and former aide Claire DeMatteis. "He knew from a very young age that family is everything."[372]

The Bidens' home church at St. Joseph's wasn't large enough for the expected attendance at Beau's memorial service, so they held a service at St. Anthony of Padua in Wilmington's Little Italy.[373] St. Anthony's building had a storied history. The church began holding services on Christmas Day 1924 at a temporary location; the land was bought in 1925. It opened with its first mass in March 1926.[374] It took two decades to finally complete, with the barrel vault being finished in 1948. The bronze doors were installed in 1966, designed by architect Leon N. Fagnani and sculpted by Egidio Giaroli.[375] "Little by little as they could afford it, the first of the lateral chapels, the columns, the arches, the lateral ceiling, small windows and medalions have been completed," historian Frank Zebley noted.[376]

In the aftermath of Beau's death, flags went to half-staff around the state.[377] Beau's body laid in state in Legislative Hall and at St. Anthony's, and the Biden family met everyone, standing for hours in the receiving line to hug, shake hands and listen to stories and memories of a life gone too early. Campaign volunteers, classmates, coworkers, national guard veterans, all turned out to surround the family in their pain and loss.[378]

The family arrived at 10:40 a.m. the day of the service. Joe, the man who had lost his daughter, son and wife, bowed his head while holding Beau's daughter's hand and kissing his widow on the head. Joe entered the church before the public wake for a final moment with his son, kneeling at Beau's casket, covered in the red, white and blue of the American flag. His right hand rested on the casket, his left braced his forehead, his eyes scrunched in pain. A rosary hung around his left wrist.[379]

Hunter and Ashley spoke, sharing memories of their brother. President Obama delivered the eulogy and then stepped down and approached Joe. They hugged, body to body, Obama's eyes closed, and they held each other tight. Joe kissed Barack on the cheek, and then Barack returned the kiss.[380]

St. Anthony of Padua Catholic Church, seen here in 1940. Beau Biden's memorial service was held here, as the Bidens' home church could not hold the number of mourners who attended. *Delaware Public Archives.*

Beau Biden lay in state in Legislative Hall. Pictured here in 1933, it is home to the Delaware House and Senate chambers, as well as legislative offices. *Delaware Public Archives.*

A solemn moment between friends: Barack hugs Joe during Beau's funeral mass at St. Anthony of Padua Catholic Church after delivering the eulogy. *Barack Obama Presidential Library.*

Beau Biden's grave sits feet from the location of the graves of his mother, sister, and grandparents'. *Dan Shortridge.*

Beau was laid to rest in the cemetery at St. Joseph's on the Brandywine, fifteen feet away from the graves of his mother and sister.[381]

In the months after Beau's passing, the family returned home to Delaware, spending a week in August at the Lake House. Joe spent his time doing physical labor and keeping the house and its grounds up to snuff. "It felt good to work the property," he remembered." I got out the chainsaw and took down some dead trees, replaced failing lightbulbs, power-washed the stucco walls. I had to call a contractor to get an estimate for installing a new tin roof on the tiny outbuilding by the lake where we kept the fishing poles."[382]

A year after Beau died, the national guard named its National Guard/ Reserve Center after him. About five hundred people gathered at the complex, many still grieving, for the commemoration, a testament to Beau's sacrifice. The center had opened in 2014 as a 106,000-square-foot home for the headquarters of the Air and Army National Guard and the U.S. Navy Reserve; now, it would be named after a Biden. Beau was a "First State treasure," a plaque mounted on the building reads. Joe, Governor Jack Markell and General Frank Vavala shared memories and stories of Beau's life

Biden poses with Lieutenant Colonel Timothy Hoyle after naming the Delaware National Guard headquarters building after Army Major Beau Biden in 2016. *U.S. Air National Guard.*

and service. "Like so many Delawareans who walk through the doors of this building, Beau answered the call," said Markell, commander-in-chief of the Delaware National Guard. He recalled a line from Isaiah that is represented in a Pentagon painting: "When God asks, 'Whom shall I send? Who will go for us?' Isaiah answered, 'Here I am. Send me.' So, too, did Beau."[383]

18

FAITH AND FAMILY

Religion is central to Joe Biden's identity. Catholicism was part and parcel of how he was raised, influencing his early outlook as well as his politics. His education, his family traditions and his worship practice were all intensely and personally Catholic in a way that has shaped his actions over the last eight decades. The rituals are soothing. He counts the rosary, describing it almost like a form of meditation. "Mass is a place I go to be by myself, even in the middle of the crowd. I always feel alone, just me and God," Biden said.

There's a family side to his faith as well:

> When I pray, I find myself not only praying to God, but praying to Neilia and my mom to intercede with God for me. It's a way of reminding myself that they are still a part of me, still inside me. And in the first few hours after we lost Beau, I began to talk to him, too.[384]

Jill says Joe's religion illuminates his life. "The Kierkegaard quote, 'Faith sees best in the dark,' seems to be written on his heart. Religion is his internal lantern, and he moves by its light, no matter how dark or difficult the terrain."[385] Those traditions and belief systems are carried on through the Biden children. Hunter recalled learning the Hail Mary not from the nuns or priests but from his grandmother. "She'd lie with us and scratch our backs while she told us stories about our mommy and what a wonderful and amazing human being she was," he remembered. "When she saw that our eyelids were heavy and about to shut, she would recite, aloud, three Hail Marys and one Our Father."[386]

For his part, Joe says the thread that ties his public service to his upbringing "was this notion of the cardinal sin [that] a government, an individual, a corporation, a business, a father, a parent can commit is to abuse the power they have, whether it is psychological, physical, financial, or political."[387] He describes himself "as much a cultural Catholic as I am a theological Catholic. My idea of self, of family, of community, of the wider world comes straight from my religion. It's not so much the Bible, the beatitudes, the Ten Commandments, the sacraments, or the prayers I learned. It's the culture. The nuns are one of the reasons I'm still a practicing Catholic."[388]

Since he is only the second Catholic president, Biden's sole example in office is John F. Kennedy, who was elected a full sixty years prior. His religion was a key point in the 2020 election cycle, "leaving no doubts about where his roots lie and what sustains him," Villanova theology professor Massimo Faggioli noted.[389] But his Catholicism was shaped by the old structure of nuns and religious orders and parochial schools that have been in decline for years. Still, America has seen a vice president and president who regularly attends mass, not to win political points but because he has done so every week over the course of his life.[390]

An aide kept a schedule of nearby Catholic services in Washington, D.C., so that when Joe's appearances on the Sunday talk shows ended, she could drive him to mass. Biden later told that aide, Margaret Aitken, "Something's going to happen to you someday. It's going to just—it's going to drop you to your knees. It's going to knock you down. And you have a choice at that time. You could either blame God or you could turn towards God for help. And I chose to turn towards God for help."[391]

After his election was certified in December 2020, Biden delivered a speech citing the prayer by St. Francis of Assisi: "May this moment give us the strength to rebuild this house of ours upon a rock that can never be washed away, as in the prayer of Saint Francis, for where there is discord, union, where there is doubt, faith, where there is darkness, light. This is who we are as a nation. This is the America we love."[392]

Still, Biden has faced opposition due to his religion, especially in the early years of his political career. In 1972, he met with state senator Curtis Steen of Dagsboro, a conservative Democrat, on U.S. 113 to campaign. Steen told Biden of a rumor that he was Catholic. It was true, Biden replied. Steen responded with an expletive. "But, senator, my wife's a Presbyterian," Joe said. "We'll just have to go with that," Steen answered.[393]

Both Neilia and Jill are Presbyterians, in fact. Jill became a member of her local church at age sixteen, near her family's home in Willow Grove, Pennsylvania.[394]

Today, the Biden family's church is St. Joseph's on the Brandywine in northern New Castle County. Also affectionately called St. Joe's, it owes its start—as do many places in Delaware—to the moneyed du Pont family. The congregation began in the home of Mrs. Victor du Pont, with mass said by Reverend Patrick Kenney prior to the 1840s. In 1841, the main church building was opened with assistance from the du Ponts, who bought the land and lent stonemasons to erect it on company time. A du Pont also provided the bell tower equipment.

The church was built from stone and covered in stucco that was then painted yellow. The building grew steadily through the years, in 1848, 1878, 1941 and 1950. Renovations inside were carried out in 1894, 1941, 1974, 1994, 2022 and 2023. Over the years, the congregation has put in new pews, windows, marble aisles and statuary. A pipe organ was also installed. In the late 1800s, the church received electricity, which allowed for a midnight mass to be held at Christmas. Outside, two separate areas make up the cemetery, the older section close to the church and a more modern area across Old Church Road. The oldest gravestone dates to 1844.

St. Joseph's on the Brandywine is the Biden family's church, and it is where three members of Joe's immediate family—Neilia, Naomi and Beau—have been laid to rest. *Delaware Public Archives.*

At the church's 1894 consecration, which featured the blessing of three altars and four statues from Germany, a Jesuit priest from Baltimore declared, "Let our faith be shown by charity, good works, alms deeds, prayer and good works. Let us pray for those outside of the church. Pray for those who are groping in the darkness for faith." That summer, a Wilmington newspaper remarked, "the Church has been transformed into one of the prettiest houses of worship in the diocese."[395]

DuPont recognized that helping its workers in the off hours would make for happier employees on the job, and many were Catholic, Irish and Italian. St. Joe's was the site of the first parochial school in the area (also funded by a du Pont), opened in 1850, which helped educate the workers' children; it was closed in 1972. The church was consecrated in 1894, then the largest Catholic church in Delaware. But when DuPont moved its powder works away from the area in the 1930s, its population began to decline, and it was feared the church would close. Delaware recovered, however, and new congregants came from across the northern part of the county. By the 1970s, a revitalized St. Joseph's was a symbol of "continuity for the Catholic faith in Delaware," historians concluded.[396]

Saint Joseph's was founded in the 1840s and has grown over the years. It was first a help to DuPont workers and then a symbol of the Catholic community. *Dan Shortridge.*

Wilmington attorney Joseph A.L. Errigo, who penned a history of the church, wrote, "The history of St. Joseph's is indeed a story of courage and sacrifice. Across its pages flash the names of mighty men and women—men and women of God. Down through the years these names come to us—increasing in stature as time passes on—priests and nuns of God who possessed that all important gift of perseverance."[397]

Joe also often attends mass at St. Edmond's Catholic Church in Rehoboth Beach. St. Edmond's traces its history to 1905, when the diocese purchased land in Rehoboth for a church. Initially, officials built a rectory, chapel and two cottages, the latter used as a summer retreat for the Sisters of St. Francis. A new church was later built and opened in 1906; it was named after St. Agnes. The building was moved away from the ocean after storms in 1914 and 1918.

St. Edmond's, the new church, was opened at a cost of $50,000 in Rehoboth Beach in 1940 to make room for the growing Catholic population in the area. "With the influx of all-year residents and a large gain in summer visitors, [St. Agnes-by-the-Sea] had proved too small for the number of worshippers who sought to attend," a Wilmington newspaper reported. A school was opened there in 1954 and operated until 1969, and the original St. Agnes building was razed after the storm of 1962. St. Edmond's celebrated its diamond jubilee in 2014–15.[398]

Religious traditions also intertwine inextricably with family traditions in the Biden household. For Christmas Eve, the family, for many years, has

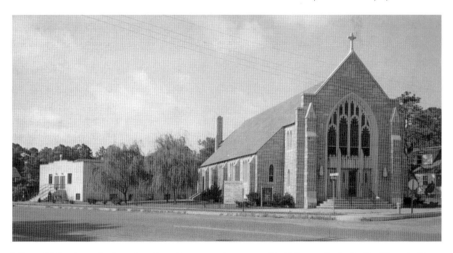

When Biden is at the beaches, he often attends mass at St. Edmond's Catholic Church. It was opened in 1940 to accommodate the area's burgeoning Catholic population. *Delaware Public Archives.*

Proud grandparents Joe and Jill pose for a photograph with their granddaughter Naomi Biden Neal and her husband, Peter Neal, on the South Lawn in 2022. *White House.*

gone to the children's mass at St. Joseph's on the Brandywine, which includes a Santa visit. And then they return to Jill and Joe's home for a large meal, complete with candles, wreaths and small gifts. The parents sleep in their rooms—"though they haven't lived with us for decades," Jill says—and the grandkids fill the basement with laughter. Christmas morning sees everyone open presents, with breakfast sandwiches for the road as they head out to visit their other parents and grandparents. "The house always sounds so quiet after everyone leaves," Jill wistfully recalls.

On a simpler note, the Bidens make sure to have dinner together every Sunday when they're home. "It's been that way for twenty-five years," Joe said.[399]

And in 2009, their first year in the vice president's residence, Joe and Jill began inviting patients from Walter Reed into their home before Thanksgiving. The patents and their family members joined them for a meal to remember, but "in the candlelight, we were all just families, telling stories," Jill recalls.[400]

A SHORT-LIVED RETIREMENT

J oe left Washington in January 2017 as a fully private citizen for the first time in forty-odd years. He was no longer an elected official and had no plans to reinvolve himself in politics. The pain of Beau's death, the need to focus on his family, were still too great and too important. Aboard the Washington Wilmington train route, an Amtrak staff member stopped by to check tickets. Joe sorted through his paper copies, Jill at his right. Across the table was U.S. representative Lisa Blunt Rochester, her e-ticket at the ready.[401]

In the two years after leaving the vice presidency, Joe, who had a simple income before joining the administration, wrote books and gave speeches, earning $15.6 million. His speaking fees were up to $234,000. The family gave $1.25 million to charity. The Beau Biden Foundation for the Protection of Children, set up in honor of Beau, held a golf and tennis tournament at the Wilmington Country Club to raise funds, with Barack Obama making a surprise appearance.[402]

Roughly a year and a half after leaving Washington, the Bidens pulled up to a rest stop on a stretch of I-95. They left with the complex bearing their name. Crowds came to witness the former vice president, Jill, Valerie and Ashley thank the state for the honor, with Joe declaring, "You've never stopped welcoming me home, our family home."

"We've been fortunate enough to travel the whole country and most of the world, and we've received a few accolades along the way," Joe said at the event, near Christiana. "But this is one of the most meaningful things that has happened to our family." State representative Gerald Brady, who sponsored

From left to right: Valerie, Jill, Ashley and Joe Biden in front of the newly named Biden Welcome Center along I-95 in New Castle County in 2018. *Office of Governor John Carney.*

the renaming bill, said the Biden family are true Delaware ambassadors to the rest of the country and the world.

The welcome center, located in the median on I-95, was built in 1964, and grew to see three million travelers stop in each year. It was torn down and rebuilt in 2010 over the course of ten months. Contractor EDiS Company said it was one of the worst winters in Delaware, with ninety-nine days of lost time. The new building has forty-two thousand square feet of dining and travel shopping space.[403]

There were also moments of solemn pride for the Bidens' home state. Of the many ships carrying the name *Delaware* in the service of the nation, the first was a twenty-four-gun frigate built in 1776. It unfortunately did not last long, as it was seized by British sailors in 1777. Ships named *Delaware* sailed in the Revolutionary War, the U.S. Civil War and World War I. The final *Delaware* was decommissioned in 1923 and scrapped in 1924; for three-quarters of a century, no naval vessel carried the name. That changed in 2000, when the new USS *Delaware*, SSN 791, a nuclear fast-attack submarine, set sail during the COVID-19 pandemic. While the formal commissioning ceremony was postponed that year—five thousand people were expected to attend in-person—a retrospective ceremony did take place in 2022 in Wilmington, attended by the Bidens.

Jill Biden was named the ship's sponsor, a signal honor from the U.S. Navy. For the keel-laying ceremony in 2016, she brought along her grandson Hunter, Beau's son, who "loves all things military," she said. "He was the one I wanted by my side." They watched as her initials were welded into the sub's keel. At the 2022 ceremony, she gave the command to call the crew.[404]

But the new president could not be trusted with the country. As Joe watched the new administration take shape and make awful decision after awful decision, his mind shifted to imagine what would have been—and what still could be. After the white supremacist rally in Charlottesville, Virginia, in 2017, Biden took to the pages of the *Atlantic*. "When it comes to race in America, hope doesn't travel alone. It's shadowed by a long trail of violence and hate. In Charlottesville, that long trail emerged once again into plain view not only for America, but for the whole world to see," he wrote.[405] He made the fateful decision to enter politics again and run, one final time, for the White House.

Then, amid a presidential campaign, the pandemic came, and the country collapsed in on itself. Large public events were replaced with videoconferencing. Masks supplanted open grins, and "social distancing" became a critical phrase. At the Biden house, staff members Annie

President Biden and First Lady Jill Biden inspect the periscope aboard the USS *Delaware*. It was the seventh naval ship to be named after the First State. *U.S. Navy.*

Tomasini, Stephen Goepfert, Ashley Williams and Anthony Bernal formed a "pod" and voluntarily isolated themselves as the staff members who would come in contact with Joe and Jill. "Their efforts were herculean," Valerie said later. His home that summer was "as solemn and secluded as an abbey," reporter Evan Osnos wrote. The cottage out front was a headquarters for the Secret Service.[406]

Instead of a national campaign, Biden ran a Delaware-based one. He met with Kamala Harris at the Hotel DuPont after her selection as his running mate. A late July event at a New Castle preschool drew reporters to talk about economics, each of them fully masked and separated in cardboard rings to ensure proper distancing. Osnos called it a "simulacrum of a campaign event that resembled a scene from an avant-garde play: no crowds, no rope lines, just a scattering of reporters." Aides met in a ballroom at the Chase Center, all masked, with no food allowed in and Plexiglass dividers between their desks.[407]

USS *Delaware* sailors line up with the president and the First Lady after its 2022 commissioning commemoration ceremony in Wilmington. Jill Biden was the vessel's sponsor. *U.S. Navy.*

The Chase Center was transformed from its origins as a World War II–era shipbuilding complex along the riverfront into an arts exhibition space and then into an events and meetings venue. It combines with the Westin Hotel to offer ninety thousand square feet of exhibition and meeting space.[408]

The Biden-Harris campaign also turned to the Queen on Wilmington's Market Street, which was closed for the pandemic, for multiple events, including news conferences, commercial tapings and interviews. The building's history dates to 1789, when it was founded as the Indian Queen Hotel and known for hosting sailors. Biden was not the first future U.S. president to visit. In 1829, Martin Van Buren stopped by a few years before defeating William Henry Harrison to win the White House. By the 1840s, it had grown to be three stories tall, which doubled the hotel's capacity.

The Queen was purchased by two banks for use as an office building in 1871, but the financial executives chose to invest in the hospitality industry and make the hotel a first-class establishment. They changed its name

Above: The Chase Center on the Riverfront in Wilmington was the site of the Biden and Harris acceptance speeches in 2020. *Dan Shortridge.*

Opposite, top: The Queen, seen in 1900, was built as a hotel in 1789. It sat closed on Wilmington's Market Street for more than five decades before reopening in 2011. *Delaware Public Archives.*

Opposite, bottom: Biden used the Queen, pictured here in 1958, just before its closure, for many events and meetings during his campaign and transition. *Delaware Public Archives.*

to the Clayton House and added two more stories. After a few decades more, it was converted to a movie theater in 1916, with total seating for two thousand people between the balcony and the main auditorium. The cinema shut down in 1959 and remained closed for fifty years, a darkened husk of memories.

The modern Queen was reborn in 2011, after several years of redevelopment work turned the former hotel into a live music venue with forty-five thousand square feet of space. It has gone through several owners since, including Philadelphia-based World Café Live and global juggernaut Live Nation.[409]

On election night, the Bidens gathered at the Lake House, Jill, Hunter, Ashley and the grandkids. The Biden tradition was for election-watching parties to be family events. Biden sat in the sunroom, the room once favored

by Beau, talking on the phone to supporters and aides around the country. Around 12:45 a.m., Biden appeared before the crowd at the Chase Center to declare his cautious optimism. "We feel good about where we are. We really do," Biden said. "I'm here to tell you tonight, we believe we're on track to win this election." Later, his aides regrouped at the Lake House in a distanced and masked election update. "Sir, you're going to win," campaign manager Jen O'Malley Dixon told him.[410]

20

THE DELAWARE BEACHES

Jack Vassalotti was walking along the Rehoboth Boardwalk in December 2018 when he saw a glint from a cufflink. He picked it up and saw the engraving with Biden's name. "I was pleasantly surprised, because I knew I could return it," he recalled. The next month, he ran into Joe at Starbucks and returned the cufflink. "He's just a great guy. The Bidens are very friendly and easy to talk to."[411]

The Bidens bought their second house on Far View Road in the North Shores community, just north of Rehoboth Beach, in the summer of 2017. "Jill and I have dreamed of being able to buy a place at the beach, a home where we can bring the whole family," Joe said at the time. "We feel very lucky that we're now able to make that happen and are looking forward to spending time with our family in the place that matters most to us in the world." They purchased the home for $2.7 million within hours of leaving the Naval Observatory, thanks in part to an $8 million multibook deal for both him and Jill. (The Sussex GOP chairman slyly made a political point: "Sussex County is a great place to have a second home, and it's a great place to retire.")[412]

Built in 2007, the home has six bedrooms and five and a half bathrooms, a gourmet kitchen, three fireplaces, outdoor showers, an elevator and built-in bookshelves. The neighborhood has experienced storm flooding and water damage, though Biden's house is elevated to protect it from major flooding.[413]

The Biden beach house, located just outside Rehoboth Beach in the community of North Shores. The wall was constructed at the request of the Secret Service for security reasons. *Dan Shortridge.*

The house had a wall built around it for security purposes; there's now a four-foot-tall fence in the front and ten-foot-tall walls around the side. Sussex County government approved a variance for the height. About $502,000 was budgeted for the five hundred feet of fence. "The property is unique in size and presented a challenge for security," Harvey Ryan, the CEO of Turnstone Holdings LLC, told the county board of adjustment. His firm was awarded the wall contract.[414]

Rehoboth has long called itself the nation's summer capital, in recognition of the symbiotic Washington, D.C.–Delaware relationship. Even before Biden was inaugurated, the Rehoboth Beach police department had an officer working with the Secret Service. The only way to access the home is through Rehoboth proper. The city has protocols in place for demonstrations, but the police chief noted that the Bidens' spur-of-the-moment drop-in visits are in the past. In 2023, Joe traveled more often to the Rehoboth house than to the Greenville lake house because of the Secret Service–overseen security upgrades. "I have no place to go when I come to Delaware, except here, right now," he said.[415]

During his presidency, Joe and Jill have often vacationed at the Rehoboth house. From Mother's Day to Labor Day 2023, he visited the beaches at least six times, according to tallies by *Cape Gazette* newspaper reporter Chris Flood. During one week in August 2023, they ate at Matt's Fish Camp in Lewes along Route 1, saw a showing of *Oppenheimer* at Movies at Midway and rode their bikes around the Gordon's Pond area of Cape Henlopen State Park. Jill visited Party Décor and More and took a class at Sea Barre Fitness in Lewes.

Cindy and Paul Lovett of Rehoboth Beach were at the theater to see *Oppenheimer* and knew something was up when they were screened at the doors and saw Secret Service agents checking under the theater's seats. Jill and Joe entered after the previews; Paul Lovett, a West Point graduate, stood when the commander-in-chief came in. The Bidens chatted with fellow moviegoers after the credits. "Paul held out his hand as the president walked by. He told Mr. Biden he was doing a good job and that he had been in the military," recalled Cindy Lovett. "The president shook his hand and said, 'My son was in the military.'"[416]

On one visit in 2021, Biden signed a "WELCOME MR. PRESIDENT" sign that had been left by the Duber family of Henlopen Acres near his home. "My heart dropped out of my body," said Charlotte Duber, aged eight. They planned to get it framed: "It's going to be someplace where everyone can see it," Charlotte said.[417]

The Bidens have also eaten breakfast at Egg in Rehoboth proper. Nicola Pizza, a noted downtown eatery that moved to Route 1, has supplied the Bidens with Italian takeout. Nick Caggiano, the owner, said he first met Biden during his 1972 campaign. "I think Joe, through the years, always had the personality," Caggiano said. "He's got the charisma."[418]

Another favorite Biden beach spot is The Ice Cream Store, just steps from the boardwalk, which once named one of its flavors after Joe. The store has photographs of Biden behind the cash register from previous visits, and in one photograph, he can be seen enjoying an Almond Joy cone. The Ice Cream Store owner Chip Hearn, who also owns the Peppers hot sauce store, praised Joe for his personal touch. "Here's the VP of the United States or a big-time senator taking the time to say hi to 19- and 20-year-olds working their butts off in the summer," Hearn reflected. "That's a big deal to them. That says a lot about what a guy he is."[419]

As a senator, Biden played a key role in building what would become the modern-day Cape Henlopen State Park. The property's history as public land dates to 1682 and a William Penn declaration known as the Warner

The Ice Cream Store has been a must-stop spot for Joe, a noted ice cream fan, during his beach vacations over the years. *Rachel Kipp.*

Grant. In the 1880s, it was used as a quarantine station for ships going up to Philadelphia. It has a long history as a military facility, starting in 1917 with a small naval base. The first gun was installed on the point in 1918. A coast guard station was built during the interwar period. In 1940, during World War II, the U.S. Army started building Fort Miles, leading to what would be 250 buildings plus 16 underground facilities. After the war, it was used as a recreation area, rocketry test site and Soviet sub listening location.

The federal government started handing over the land to the State of Delaware in 1964, starting with 543 acres as Cape Henlopen State Park. Fort Miles closed in 1992, and the final piece of land was transferred to the state in 1996. The 17-acre parcel of land was used by the U.S. Navy as a training center. The building was named after Biden, now called the Biden Environmental Training Center, for his work bringing the land back to state ownership.

"Three centuries ago," Biden said at the transfer event, "William Penn granted the land at Cape Henlopen to Edward Warner, a local official, to be held in trust for use by the citizens of this area....He had the foresight

The Biden Environmental Training Center at Cape Henlopen State Park is seen here undergoing renovations in early 2024. *Dan Shortridge.*

Browseabout Books in Rehoboth Beach has been a favorite stop for the Bidens. "Hi, I'm Jill's husband," Joe said while greeting visitors to Jill's book signing there in 2019. *Dan Shortridge.*

and wisdom to set aside this pristine area for the enjoyment of all."[420] In 2022, Biden visited a bench that was placed at Herring Point in honor of Beau, prior to taking a spill while riding his bike at Cape Henlopen. He took photographs with a few beachgoers and chatted with parents and kids.[421]

While vacationing at the beaches, the Bidens have been frequent visitors to Browseabout Books, one of Delaware's preeminent independent bookstores that sits on Rehoboth Avenue. In 2019, Jill Biden signed hundreds of copies of her autobiography at Browseabout in a marathon session, taking photographs with everyone who wanted one. The fans lined up outside the doors at 6:00 a.m., four hours before the signing began. Joe shook hands with everyone, saying, "Hi, I'm Jill's husband." (Shoppers were reported to have said, "Let's do our Christmas shopping, and if we happen to see Joe, great.")

Joe used to stop by Browseabout after the end of the Obama administration for newspapers and coffee after church services. "We're not fan-girling. We want everyone to feel welcome," said Jessie Jones, a Browseabout staff member. "Now, people in the store, that's a different

Books by both Bidens sit in alphabetical position on the shelf at Browseabout Books. *Dan Shortridge.*

story." Browseabout once put up a display complete with Biden swag and books—earrings, mugs, coloring books, an action figure, socks and a scented candle (orange Gatorade, a favorite flavor).[422]

"I'm sure we will see him more often," said the bookstore's general manager Susan Kehoe in 2017. "I hope so." Like Hearn, she praised Biden's appeal and friendliness. "He sort of defies party lines....I think no matter what side of the political fence you are, you kind of just have to love Joe."[423]

21

ONE OF US

At the time of this writing, Joe Biden has been president for just over three years. Despite the torturous divided Congress, his administration has reversed many policies of the previous administration and created entirely new ones. He has expanded overtime eligibility, grown access to birth control, signed a gun safety law, delved into renewable energy sources, reinforced anti-redlining measures in mortgage lending, slashed junk fees, cleaned up the nation's electoral transition system, aided the shrinking Colorado River and worked to eliminate much of the country's student loan debt.[424]

For someone who long dreamed of leading our country and sitting in the White House, Biden's election came as something of a surprise to many Americans. He was a popular vice president who stepped back at the height of his popularity. He had waged several unsuccessful battles for the presidency before. And he was running in one of the most colorful election cycles in American history.

But for Delawareans, who know Joe most closely, his victory was not a bolt from above. His sacrifices and sense of duty are well known here. What America knows about Biden is primarily his age, vice presidency, long Senate tenure and personal tragedy, mainly Beau's loss. Most American voters do not know about his family's first loss, that of Neilia's talents and Naomi's sweetness. They do not know the story of his county council tenure or his Senate election or of his time at Archmere or the University of Delaware. They may have heard fragments about his law career, but they were not

Top: President Biden visits Arlington National Cemetery's Section 60, where the dead from the nation's most recent wars have been put to rest, in 2021. *U.S. Army.*

Bottom: Biden speaks to members of the armed forces in Japan in 2011. As a military father, soldiers, sailors, airmen and marines have always been close to Joe's heart. *U.S. Air Force.*

there when he taught law school. Some of those moments date back more than five decades, yet they forged Joe along the way and from those times forward.

That is the Joe Biden Delaware knows. The Joe we saw for decades, the Joe we shaped and created, is a fighter. He is a triumphant, happy warrior, a compassionate sharer of kindness. He has lived through our pain, and we have lived through his. He has taken us through good times and bad, upstate and downstate, from the state line to the Delaware Bay. He has cycled with us at Cape Henlopen, dined with us at restaurants galore, attended our chicken festivals and party rallies and knocked on our doors. He has been one of us.

And despite his current residence in the nation's capital, he remains one of us. From his childhood to his grandchildren, Joe is a Delawarean through and through. His passion for the First State's people and places has changed both his political career and his life. And we will be here to have his back no matter where he goes or what he does.

NOTES

Preface

1. News Journal, *Joe's Journey*, 122.
2. Osnos, *Joe Biden*, 60.
3. Cohen, *Only in Delaware*, 253.
4. Cramer, *What It Takes*, 254.
5. H. Biden, *Beautiful Things*, 52.
6. Schreckinger, *The Bidens*, 108.
7. Cohen, *Only in Delaware*, 243.
8. Ibid., 363.
9. Schreckinger, *The Bidens*, 123–24.
10. Witcover, *Joe Biden*, 212.

Chapter 1

11. Weitzman, *What's the Matter with Delaware?*, 160.
12. Witcover, *Joe Biden*, 17.
13. Joe Biden, *Promises to Keep*, 5–6.
14. Witcover, *Joe Biden*, 18.
15. Mike Lang, "Holy Rosary Parish in Claymont Marks 100 Years with Mass, Dinner and Special Guests." *Dialog*, May 17, 2022, www.thedialog.org.
16. "Work on Claymont Parish School to Start in Spring," *Journal-Every Evening*, February 9, 1949, 1–4.

17. Joe Biden, *Promises to Keep*, 8.

18. Ibid., 7–9.

19. Witcover, *Joe Biden*, 30.

20. Joe Biden, *Promises to Keep*, 14.

21. Ibid., 41.

22. Joe Biden, *Promises to Keep*, 7, 14; Richard L. Gaw, "At United School, an Energy of Togetherness," *News Journal*, December 31, 2009, CT13.

23. Joe Biden, *Promises to Keep*, 11.

24. Antonio Prado, "The Two Become One: Pope John Paul II School Born from St. Helena's and Holy Rosary," *Hockessin Community News*, August 28, 2008, www.delawareonline.com.

25. Gaw, "United School," CT13.

26. Claymont Historical Society, "Claymont History," www.claymonthistoricalsociety.org/claymont-de-history.html.

27. Jeff Mordock, "A 'Game-Changer' for Claymont," *News Journal*, November 13, 2015. www.delawareonline.com.

28. Beth Miller, "Climate Seems Right for Claymont Renaissance," *News Journal*, May 10, 2015, A1-2.

29. Mordock, "Game-Changer."

Chapter 2

30. Joe Biden, *Promises to Keep*, 6–7.

31. Archmere Academy, "Affording Archmere," www.archmereacademy.com/admissions/affording-archmere.

32. Joe Biden, *Promises to Keep*, 18–19.

33. National Park Service, "Archmere," National Register of Historic Places registration form, July 30, 1992.

34. Stephen J. Rossey, "The Estate of Archmere: A Personal View," 1984, rev. ed. 2001, digital.hagley.org/raskob-arch-personal.

35. National Park Service, "Archmere," National Register of Historic Places registration form, July 30, 1992.

36. Ann Marie Linnabery, "City Native Became Financial Wizard," *Lockport Union-Sun & Journal*, May 24, 2014, www.lockportjournal.com.

37. National Park Service, "Archmere," National Register of Historic Places registration form, July 30, 1992.

38. Joe Biden, *Promises to Keep*, 23; Witcover, *Joe Biden*, 27.

39. Robert Shogan, "Biden Struggles with Tragedy in '88 Decision," *Los Angeles Times*, February 8, 1987, www.latimes.com.

40. CBS News, "We're All Using It as a Huge Flex," November 13, 2020, www.cbsnews.com.
41. "Archmere Closes With 8-0 Mark," *Journal-Every Evening*, November 12, 1960, 24.
42. Witcover, *Joe Biden*, 24.
43. Cramer, *What It Takes*, 260.
44. Joe Biden, *Promises to Keep*, 23.
45. Witcover, *Joe Biden*, 24.
46. Edward L. Kenney, "Biden Has Kept in Touch with His Claymont Roots," *News Journal*, August 27, 2008, 15.
47. Witcover, *Joe Biden*, 30.
48. Cramer, *What It Takes*, 260.
49. Witcover, *Joe Biden*, 33; Joe Biden, *Promises to Keep*, 31.
50. John A. Monroe, *The University of Delaware: A History* (Newark: University of Delaware, 1986), n.p. https://sites.udel.edu/uarm/the-university-of-delaware/.
51. "Freshmen Elect Archmere Graduate," *Evening Journal*, November 16, 1961, 32.
52. Shogan, "Biden Struggles."
53. Witcover, *Joe Biden*, 31–32, 61; H. Biden, *Beautiful Things*, 77.
54. Joe Biden, *Promises to Keep*, 44.
55. Witcover, *Joe Biden*, 30.
56. Christina Jedra, "Wilmington Names Pool After Joe Biden, Former Lifeguard," *News Journal*, June 26, 2017, www.delawareonline.com.
57. Travis M. Andrews, "Joe Biden Recalls Lessons Learned as the Only White Lifeguard at City Pool in 1962," *Washington Post*, June 27, 2017, www.washingtonpost.com.

Chapter 3

58. Joe Biden, *Promises to Keep*, 31–33.
59. Witcover, *Joe Biden*, 39.
60. Jane Harriman, "Biden: Hope for Democratic Party in '72?" *Evening Journal*, November 11, 1970, 3.
61. "Neilia Hunter to Marry J.R. Biden," *Evening Journal*, March 29, 1966, 20; Abby Weiss, "The One: Joe Biden's 1st Wife Neilia Biden Shaped His Life, Career While at Syracuse," *Daily Orange*, February 22, 2022, www.dailyorange.com.
62. Witcover, *Joe Biden*, 39.

63. Celia Cohen, "William T. Quillen, 1935–2016," *Delaware Grapevine*, August 22, 2016. www.delawaregrapevine.com.

64. Witcover, *Joe Biden*, 51.

65. Joe Biden, *Promises to Keep*, 41.

66. Harriman, "Biden: Hope for Democratic Party," 3.

67. "20 in State Pass Bar Examinations," *Evening Journal*, November 2, 1968, 11.

68. "The Terrys to Welcome New Lawyers," *Morning News*, December 14, 1968, 13.

69. Joe Biden, *Promises to Keep*, 38.

70. Maureen Milford, "Law Practice Is a Far Cry from Its Roots," *News Journal*, September 25, 1988, 19.

71. Prickett, Jones & Elliott, "About the Firm," www.prickett.com/about-the-firm/.

72. Joe Biden, *Promises to Keep*, 42.

73. Witcover, *Joe Biden*, 54.

74. "Moooving Story Lightens Sentence," *Morning News*, June 14, 1969, 2.

75. "Tried to Shape Up, Got Four Years Anyhow," *Evening Journal*, October 2, 1971.

76. Witcover, *Joe Biden*, 55.

77. Jeff Mordock, "Sid Balick, a Giant in Politics and Law, Will be Remembered Thursday," *News Journal*, June 21, 2017, www.delawareonline.com.

78. Witcover, *Joe Biden*, 55–56.

79. "Penn Central Sued in 2 '67 Accidents," *Evening Journal*, October 3, 1969, 12.

80. "Bacon Center Houseparents Sue State," *Morning News*, December 29, 1971, 17.

81. Shogan, "Biden Struggles."

82. Mordock, "Sid Balick."

83. "St. Bernard's Rescuer Saved," *Morning News*, March 5, 1969, 2.

84. Schreckinger, *The Bidens*, 109.

85. Joe Biden, *Promises to Keep*, 42–43.

86. National Governors Association, "Gov. Charles L. Terry," www.nga.org; State of Delaware, "Official Results of General Election, 1968," April 30, 1969, elections.delaware.gov.

87. National Governors Association, "Gov. Russell W. Peterson," www.nga.org.

88. Cohen, *Only in Delaware*, 170, 188–79, 191.

89. Celia Cohen, "A Man of His Time," *Delaware Grapevine*, February 24, 2011, www.delawaregrapevine.com.

90. "Sherman Tribbitt Obituary," *Delaware State News*, August 18, 2010, www.legacy.com.

91. Cohen, *Only in Delaware*, 212.

Chapter 4

92. "Democrat Forum Elects Lindh," *Morning News*, November 13, 1969, 18.

93. Witcover, *Joe Biden*, 57.

94. Joe Biden, *Promises to Keep*, 50.

95. "Biden in Bid for County Council Seat," *Evening Journal*, May 22, 1970, 9.

96. "Biden Blasts County Brass on Crime," *Evening Journal*, August 10, 1970, 22.

97. "Candidate Wants Garbage Overhaul," *Evening Journal*, October 28, 1970, 8.

98. Tom Warwick, "County Council Election Battles Intensify," *Morning News*, October 13, 1970, 17.

99. "Lawrence T. Messick," *News-Journal*, supplement, October 24, 1970, 14; Parsell Funeral Homes, "Lawrence T. Messick, Sr.," www.parsellfuneralhomes.com.

100. Biden Owens, *Growing Up Biden*, 88.

101. Patricia Talorico and Meredith Newman, "Joe Biden Lost His Wife and Baby Daughter 50 Years Ago. It Changed the Course of His Life," *News Journal*, December 14, 2022, www.delawareonline.com.

102. Al Cartwright, "Biden Wanted Wife to Organize Capital Office," *Evening Journal*, December 22, 1972, 3.

103. "2 School Votes Favor Daniello; Rest All GOP," *Evening Journal*, October 30, 1970, 29.

104. State of Delaware, "Official Results of General Election, 1970," www.elections.delaware.gov.

105. Harriman, "Biden: Hope for Democratic Party," 3.

106. "Bockman to Spurn Topel Reform Unit," *Evening Journal*, November 20, 1970, 34.

107. Witcover, *Joe Biden*, 62.

108. "Shell Plans Face Zoning Challenge," *Evening Journal*, January 27, 1971, 3.

109. "Biden to Open Special Office for Constituency Contacts," *Evening Journal*, January 20, 1971, 30.

110. Marilyn Mather, "Coordinated Development Is County Aim," *Morning News*, May 13, 1971, 2.

111. "State Lack of Mass Transit Blamed on Highways Unit," *Evening Journal*, October 13, 1971, 38.

Chapter 5

112. National Governors Association, "Gov. James Caleb Boggs," www. nga.org.

113. Joe Biden, *Promises to Keep*, 54.

114. Biden Owens, *Growing Up Biden*, 89.

115. Al Cartwright, "They All Thought They Could Beat Cale Boggs," *Evening Journal*, March 29, 1972, 3.

116. National Governors Association, "Boggs."

117. Levingston, *Barack and Joe*, 17.

118. Jack Nolan, "Democrats Seek Status Unquo," *Evening Journal*, March 23, 1971, 21.

119. News Journal, *Joe's Journey*, 37.

120. Joe Biden, *Promises to Keep*, 57–58.

121. William P. Frank, "Angry Democrats Have New Look," *Evening Journal*, July 24, 1941, 1.

122. Joe Biden, *Promises to Keep*, 58–60; Witcover, *Joe Biden*, 469.

123. Bob Frump, "Too Early for Senate Bid, But Biden Considering Try," *Evening Journal*, September 27, 1971, 3.

124. Ron Williams, "Biden Struts Like Candidate for U.S. Senate," *Evening Journal*, September 1, 1971, 34.

125. "Straw-in-the-Wind Time," *Morning News*, October 7, 1971, 10.

126. Jeff Mordock, "Era Ends as Dupont Sells Its Hotel," *News Journal*, January 31, 2017, www.delawareonline.com.

127. Hagley Museum and Library, "Hotel du Pont Historical Files," 2014, www.hagley.org; "7,272 Silver Pieces for Hotel," *Evening Journal*, May 21, 1912, 7.

128. Mordock, "Era Ends."

129. Witcover, *Joe Biden*, 72.

130. Joe Biden, *Promises to Keep*, xvii.

131. Ibid., 61; Osnos, *Joe Biden*, 36.

132. Cohen, *Only in Delaware*, 204.

133. Biden Owens, *Growing Up Biden*, 98.

134. Ibid., 92; Witcover, *Joe Biden*, 72–73.

135. Joe Biden, *Promises to Keep*, 63–64; Biden Owens, *Growing Up Biden*, 92.

136. Alex Vuocolo, "On the Cusp of Retirement, Rich Heffron Looks Back at a Long Career," *Delaware Business Times*, January 26, 2018; Witcover, *Joe Biden*, 76.

137. Bill Frank, "Is Joe Biden Just a Young Cale Boggs?" *Morning News*, March 22, 1972, 10.

138. Bill Frank, "If Boggs Is the Irresistible Object, Then…," *Morning News*, June 9, 1972, 36.

139. Witcover, *Joe Biden*, 87.

140. Schreckinger, *The Bidens*, 26.

141. Joe Biden, *Promises to Keep*, 63; Schreckinger, *The Bidens*, 29.

142. Biden Owens, *Growing Up Biden*, 93.

143. Joe Biden, *Promises to Keep*, 71.

144. Witcover, *Joe Biden*, 76.

145. Norman Lockman, "Biden Switches to 'Dear Old Dad' Line," *Evening Journal*, October 28, 1972, 19.

146. Advertisement, *Evening Journal*, October 30, 1972, 12.

147. Advertisement, *Evening Journal*, October 28, 1972, 4.

148. Advertisement, *Evening Journal*, October 17, 1972, 7.

149. Biden Owens, *Growing Up Biden*, 107.

150. Joe Biden, *Promises to Keep*, 67, 73.

151. Biden Owens, *Growing Up Biden*, 108.

152. Schreckinger, *The Bidens*, 27.

153. State of Delaware, "Official Results of General Election, 1972," www.elections.delaware.gov.

154. Terry Zintl and Norman Lockman, "State Elects the Youngest U.S. Senator," *Evening Journal*, November 8, 1972, 1–4.

155. Cohen, *Only in Delaware*, 207.

156. Talorico and Newman, "Biden Lost His Wife and Baby Daughter 50 Years Ago."

157. Witcover, *Joe Biden*, 89.

158. Joe Biden, *Promises to Keep*, xix–xx.

Chapter 6

159. Witcover, *Joe Biden*, 91.

160. Joe Biden, *Promises to Keep*, 77–78.

161. Cartwright, "Biden Wanted," 3.

162. Witcover, *Joe Biden*, 93.

163. H. Biden, *Beautiful Things*, 11–12.

164. Carl Hamilton, "Daughter of Man in '72 Biden Crash Seeks Apology from Widowed Senator," *Newark Post*, October 30, 2008, www.newarkpostonline.com.

165. Witcover, *Joe Biden*, 94.

166. H. Biden, *Beautiful Things*, 58.

167. Cartwright, "Biden Wanted," 3.

168. Jill Biden, *Where the Light Enters*, 40–41.
169. Talorico and Newman, "Biden Lost His Wife and Baby Daughter 50 Years Ago."
170. Diocese of Wilmington, "About Catholic Cemeteries," www.cdow.org.
171. Celia Cohen, "Family Matters," *Delaware Grapevine*, August 16, 2013, www.delawaregrapevine.com.
172. Witcover, *Joe Biden*, 95–96.
173. H. Biden, *Beautiful Things*, 32, 57.
174. Joe Biden, *Promises to Keep*, 151–53.
175. H. Biden, *Beautiful Things*, 109–10.
176. Hamilton, "Daughter of Man in '72 Biden Crash Seeks Apology."
177. Witcover, *Joe Biden*, 98, 104.
178. Levingston, *Barack and Joe*, 21.
179. Schreckinger, *The Bidens*, 31; Witcover, *Joe Biden*, 98.
180. U.S. Senate, "About the Senate & the U.S. Constitution | Oath of Office," www.senate.gov.
181. Witcover, *Joe Biden*, 115.
182. Weiss, "The One."
183. Ron Williams, "Biden Weeps on Return to Sussex," *Morning News*, March 5, 1973, 3.

Chapter 7

184. Shogan, "Biden Struggles."
185. Witcover, *Joe Biden*, 108.
186. Ralph Moyed, "Biden Will Urge U.S. Homesteading," *Evening Journal*, November 9, 1973, 1.
187. Osnos, *Joe Biden*, 55.
188. Biden Owens, *Growing Up Biden*, 126.
189. Whipple, *Fight of His Life*, 8.
190. Rachel Kurzius, "8 Things We Learned about Joe Biden's Homes from the Hur Interview," *Washington Post*, March 12, 2024, www.washingtonpost.com.
191. Kevin Shalvey, "Amtrak Joe: A Brief Look at President Biden's Long History of Supporting America's Railroad," *Business Insider*, April 10, 2021, www.businessinsider.com.
192. Great American Stations, "Wilmington, DE (WIL)," www.greatamericanstations.com.
193. Amtrak, "Amtrak Completes Wilmington Station Renovations," October 23, 2023, ww.media.amtrak.com.

194. WHYY, "Wilmington Amtrak Station Renamed After Vice President Biden," March 19, 2011, www.whyy.org.

195. Shalvey, "Amtrak Joe."

196. Jason Hoffman, "Biden Uses His Long History with Amtrak to Put a Personal Touch on Infrastructure Push." CNN, April 30, 2021, www.cnn.com.

197. Joe Biden, *Promises to Keep*, 153; Kitty Kelley, "Death and the All-American Boy," *Washingtonian*, June 1, 1974, www.washingtonian.com.

198. Cohen, *Only in Delaware*, 325–26.

199. Weitzman, *What's the Matter with Delaware?*, 204.

200. Osnos, *Joe Biden*, 49.

201. Cohen, *Only in Delaware*, 207.

Chapter 8

202. Witcover, *Joe Biden*, 124.

203. Jill Biden, *Where the Light Enters*, 39.

204. Schreckinger, *The Bidens*, 53.

205. Jill Biden, *Where the Light Enters*, 42.

206. Ibid.; Schreckinger, *The Bidens*, 56.

207. Schreckinger, *The Bidens*, 61.

208. Witcover, *Joe Biden*, 125.

209. Biden Owens, *Growing Up Biden*, 147; Joe Biden, *Promises to Keep*, 117.

210. Schreckinger, *The Bidens*, 62.

211. Joe Biden, *Promises to Keep*, 118–19.

212. Whipple, *Fight of His Life*, 278.

213. Saint Mark's High School, "School History," www.stmarkshs.net.

214. Colonial School District, "WE Celebrate: Jill Biden—First Lady," March 5, 2021, www.colonialschooldistrict.org.

215. White House Historical Association, "Dr. Jill Biden," www.whitehousehistory.org/bios/dr-jill-biden.

216. William P. Frank, "Dr. T Visits New Psychiatric Center," *Morning News*, April 26, 1974, 18.

217. Antonio Prado, "Brandywine High School to Celebrate 50th Anniversary at Homecoming," *Community News*, October 16, 2008, www.delawareonline.com.

218. Katie Glueck, "Jill Biden Returns to Her Old Classroom to Deliver a Convention Speech," *New York Times*, August 18, 2020, www.nytimes.com.

219. White House Historical Association, "Dr. Jill Biden."

220. Whipple, *Fight of His Life*, 278–81.

Chapter 9

221. Witcover, *Joe Biden*, 139.

222. Biden Owens, *Growing Up Biden*, 155.

223. Joe Biden, *Promises to Keep*, 123; City of Dover, "Regular City Council Meeting: March 13, 1978," www.cityofdover.com

224. State of Delaware, "Official Results of General Election, 1978," www.elections.delaware.gov.

225. H. Biden, *Beautiful Things*, 69.

226. Cohen, *Only in Delaware*, 265.

227. Joe Biden, *Promises to Keep*, 135–36.

228. Witcover, *Joe Biden*, 146, 149, 153.

229. Cohen, *Only in Delaware*, 302.

230. Cathy Wolff, "Candidates Get Hot on Police Issue," *Morning News*, October 7, 1970, 26.

231. Katie Tabeling, "John Burris Awarded Delaware Chamber's Gilman Bowl," *Delaware Business Times*, November 3, 2021, www.delawarebusinesstimes.com.

232. Cohen, *Only in Delaware*, 306–7.

233. State of Delaware, "Official Results of General Election, 1984," January 16, 1985, www.elections.delaware.gov.

234. State of Delaware, "2000 General Election," November 22, 2000, www.elections.delaware.gov.

235. State of Delaware, "Official Results of General Election, 1990," March 27, 1991, www.elections.delaware.gov.

236. Paul Kiefer, "Julianne Murray Outlines Priorities as New Delaware GOP Chair," Delaware Public Media, May 6, 2023, www.delawarepublic.org.

237. "Raymond Jack Clatworthy, III," *News Journal*, December 26, 2021, www.delawareonline.com.

238. State of Delaware, "1996 Election Results," www.elections.delaware.gov.

239. State of Delaware, "2002 General Election," November 8, 2002, elections.delaware.gov.

240. "Clatworthy, III," *News Journal*.

241. Library of Congress, "Return Day," www.memory.loc.gov.

242. Ken Mammarella, "History of Return Day: From Politics to Parties, the Tradition Dates Back to 1812," Delaware Public Media, November 4, 2022, www.delawarepublic.org.
243. Joe Biden, *Promises to Keep*, 74.
244. Ron Williams, "New Faces, Same High Tones Warm Return Day's Bluster," *Morning News*, November 10, 1972, 40.
245. Schreckinger, *The Bidens*, 114.
246. Randall Chase, "Enthusiastic Crowd Welcomes Biden Home to Delaware," Associated Press, November 6, 2008, www.sandiegouniontribune.com.

Chapter 10

247. Delaware Historical Society, "Biography—Senator William V. Roth," www.dehistory.org.
248. Cohen, *Only in Delaware*, 420.
249. Ibid., 409.
250. Delaware Historical Society, "Senator William V. Roth."
251. U.S. Air Force, "Dover AFB History," www.dover.af.mil.
252. Joe Biden, *Promise Me, Dad*, 65.
253. U.S. Air Force, "AFMAO Facilities," www.mortuary.af.mil.
254. Tamara Keith, "Biden Attends the Dignified Transfer at Dover for Service Members Killed in Jordan," NPR, February 2, 2024, www.npr.org.
255. Senate Historical Office, "Edward Ed (Ted) Kaufman," Oral History Interviews, August 17–August 24, 2011, www.senate.gov.
256. Biden Owens, *Growing Up Biden*, 164.

Chapter 11

257. Biden, *Promises to Keep*, 52.
258. Schreckinger, *The Bidens*, 19.
259. Suzanne Herel, "Former Home of Joe Biden, Built in 1723, Up for Sale in North Star," *News Journal*, May 2, 2018, www.delawareonline.com.
260. Cramer, *What It Takes*, 243.
261. Ibid., 248; Biden Owens, *Growing Up Biden*, 144.
262. Reuters, "Fact Check: Image Shows Home Joe Biden Bought for $185,000 in the Mid-1970s," October 22, 2020, www.reuters.com; Schreckinger, *The Bidens*, 83–84; Cramer, *What It Takes*, 249–51; H. Biden, *Beautiful Things*, 63.

263. Joe Biden, *Promises to Keep*, 113.

264. H. Biden, *Beautiful Things*, 63; Cramer, *What It Takes*, 250–51.

265. Biden Owens, *Growing Up Biden*, 142.

266. Schreckinger, *The Bidens*, 92–93.

267. Ibid.; Cris Barrish, "Analysis: How Biden Made a Large Profit on the Sale of His House," *News Journal*, September 6, 2008, www.delawareonline.com.

268. Kurzius, "8 Things."

269. Schreckinger, *The Bidens*, 159–60.

270. Zeke Miller, "The Hur Interview Transcript Offers a Window into the Life of 'Frustrated Architect' Joe Biden," Associated Press, March 16, 2024, wwwapnews.com.

271. Amie Parnes, "Biden Finds Time for Delaware at White House," *The Hill*, April 8, 2021, www.thehill.com.

Chapter 12

272. Witcover, *Joe Biden*, 91.

273. Meredith Newman, "How Joe Biden Changed Delaware Politics," *News Journal*, November 10, 2020, 6T.

274. Charles P. Arcaro Funeral Home, "Robert A Piane," www.arcarofuneralhome.com.

275. Robin Brown, "Caterer's 'Love Works' Program: Feast for the Spirit," *News Journal*, March 27, 1989, 3.

276. Joe Biden, *Promises to Keep*, 207; Patricia Talorico, "Love, Italian Style," *News Journal*, February 8, 2024, B1.

277. Patricia Talorico, "President Biden Dines at Mrs. Robino's in Wilmington, Once Also Visited by Guy Fieri," *News Journal*, February 13, 2024, www.delawareonline.com.

278. Joe Biden, *Promises to Keep*, 38; "Henry J. Winkler, Wilmington Restaurateur," *Cape Gazette*, April 17, 2011, www.capegazette.com; "Winkler's Soon to Demolish Old Shipley House for Parking," *Journal-Every Evening*, April 2, 1957, 1; Maureen Milford, "Eatery Closes Indefinitely," *News Journal*, November 28, 1984, C10; Maureen Milford, "Food Can Be Advertised But Not Served: Old, Romantic Winkler's Restaurant Has Become the Cozy Home of an Ad Agency," *News Journal*, June 28, 1986, C1.

279. Wright & Simon, "The Simon Legacy," https://www.wrightandsimon.com/about/simon-legacy/; Christopher Maag,

"President-Elect Joe Biden's Hometown of Wilmington, Delaware Is a Hub for Secrets," NorthJersey.com, November 13, 2020, www. northjersey.com.

Chapter 13

280. H. Biden, *Beautiful Things*, 58–59.

281. Patricia Talorico, "Dog House, Charcoal Pit Founder Lous Sloan Dies at 86," *News Journal*, August 31, 2016, www.delawareonline.com; Pam George, "Louis Sloan, Founder of the Dog House and Charcoal Pit, Dies," *Delaware Today*, September 2, 2016, www.delawaretoday.com; H. Biden, *Beautiful Things*, 109.

282. H. Biden, *Beautiful Things*, 59.

283. Witcover, *Joe Biden*, 99.

284. Biden Owens, *Growing Up Biden*, 149–50.

285. H. Biden, *Beautiful Things*, 22, 65.

286. Schreckinger, *The Bidens*, 85, 115.

287. Jessica McDowell, "A Lasting Legacy: People Remember 1991 College Graduate Beau Biden," *Daily Pennsylvanian*, June 4, 2015.

288. Schreckinger, *The Bidens*, 117; Xerxes Wilson, "Delaware Is Changing the Bar Exam. Here's What That Means for Current, Future Lawyers," *News Journal*, February 21, 2023, www.delawareonline.com; H. Biden, *Beautiful Things*, 84.

289. Schreckinger, *The Bidens*, 115.

290. Celia Cohen, "Beau Biden Is Coming, and Schnee Is Sort of Going," *Delaware Grapevine*, July 23, 2004, www.delawaregrapevine.com.

291. "Tatnall School," *News Journal*, June 5, 1991, 53.

292. Schreckinger, *The Bidens*, 142; Biden, *Promise Me, Dad*, 181.

293. "New Castle County Property Transfers," *News Journal*, October 25, 2003, RE45.

294. "The Graduates of the Class of '99," *News Journal*, May 23, 1999, 11; "High School Report," *News Journal*, September 23, 2010, CT12.

295. "Delaware Women Support Joe Biden," *News Journal*, November 4, 1996, A9.

296. "Beau Biden Is Promoted to Major by Del. Guard," *News Journal*, November 7, 2011, B2.

297. Hallie Biden, "Delaware Takes Beau Biden's Quest to Protect Children Nationwide," *News Journal*, January 8, 2019, www. delawareonline.com.

298. Schreckinger, *The Bidens*, 31.

299. Joe Biden, *Promise Me, Dad*, 117.

300. H. Biden, *Beautiful Things*, 40.

301. Ibid., 60–62; Biden Owens, *Growing Up Biden*, 203.

302. H. Biden, *Beautiful Things*, 73.

303. Buhle, *If We Break*, 5; H. Biden, *Beautiful Things*, 81.

304. Witcover, *Joe Biden*, 297; Buhle, *If We Break*, 41, 44.

305. Buhle, *If We Break*, 46–47, 51; Schreckinger, *The Bidens*, 95.

306. H. Biden, *Beautiful Things*, 215, 241.

307. Joe Biden, *Promises to Keep*, 119.

308. Witcover, *Joe Biden*, 161.

309. Kate Bennett, "Ashley Biden Finds Her Voice: 'I Know My Worth,'" CNN, November 4, 2022, www.cnn.com; Buhle, *If We Break*, 29.

310. Jarek Rutz, "Wilmington Friends School to Mark 275th Anniversary," Delaware LIVE, August 23, 2023, www.delawarelive.com; Kayla Webley Adler, "Ashley Biden Knows Who She Is," *Elle*, March 28, 2023, www.elle.com; Schreckinger, *The Bidens*, 93; Bennett, "Ashley Biden Finds Her Voice."

311. Bennett, "Ashley Biden Finds Her Voice."; Adler, "Ashley Biden Knows."

312. Bennett, "Ashley Biden Finds Her Voice."

313. Adler, "Ashley Biden Knows."

Chapter 14

314. Frank, *Frank's Delaware*, 298.

315. Cohen, *Only in Delaware*, 330, 333.

316. Biden, *Promises to Keep*, 203; Witcover, *Joe Biden*, 169, 215–16; Schreckinger, *The Bidens*, 76.

317. Biden, *Promises to Keep*, 207.

318. Cohen, *Only in Delaware*, 340.

319. Biden, *Promises to Keep*, 218.

320. Biden Owens, *Growing Up Biden*, 186.

321. H. Biden, *Beautiful Things*, 75.

322. Witcover, *Joe Biden*, 238.

323. Cohen, *Only in Delaware*, 344.

324. Mark Eichmann, "Delaware Democrats Celebrate Annual Jamboree," WHYY, September 19, 2016, www.whyy.org.

325. Cohen, *Only in Delaware*, 344.

326. Witcover, *Joe Biden*, 238–39.

327. Cohen, *Only in Delaware*, 344–45; Senate Historical Office, "Edward Ed (Ted) Kaufman."

Chapter 15

328. Emily Barrett, "Before He Was Mr. President, He Was Professor Biden to His Widener Students," Widener University, Delaware Law School, January 20, 2021, www.widener.edu; Mary Allen, executive director of communications, personal communication, Widener University, February 6, 2024; "Biden Brings the Constitution to the Classroom," *Widener University School of Law Magazine*, summer 1997.
329. Levingston, *Barack and Joe*, 24.
330. Witcover, *Joe Biden*, 436.
331. Levingston, *Barack and Joe*, 62–63.
332. Celia Cohen, "Poli-Ticking," *Delaware Grapevine*, February 9, 2005, www.delawaregrapevine.com.
333. Whipple, *Fight of His Life*, 198.
334. "Biden Brings the Constitution to the Classroom," *Widener University School of Law Magazine*.
335. "Joseph Robinette Biden, Sr.," *News Journal*, September 5, 2002.
336. Biden Owens, *Growing Up Biden*, 201.
337. Delaware Courts, "The Honorable Ferris W. Wharton, Judge," www.courts.delaware.gov.
338. State of Delaware, "2006 General Election," November 16, 2006, www.elections.delaware.gov.
339. "Beau Biden: 1969–2015," *News Journal*, June 1, 2015, A4.
340. Alex Vuocolo, "State Officials Cut Ribbon on Carvel State Building Renovations," *Delaware Business Times*, October 2, 2019, www.delawarebusinesstimes.com.
341. Cris Barrish, "Del. Child Abuse Victims Notified of Settlement Payouts," *News Journal*, November 25, 2013, www.usatoday.com.
342. Mark Eichmann, "Beau Biden's Legacy of Protecting Children," WHYY, June 4, 2015, www.whyy.org.

Chapter 16

343. Levingston, *Barack and Joe*, 31, 39.
344. H. Biden, *Beautiful Things*, 89; Joe Biden, *Promise Me, Dad*, 59.

345. Joe Biden, *Promise Me, Dad*, 64–65; Levingston, *Barack and Joe*, 66; Paul Bedard, "Former McCain, Obama Aides Schmidt and Plouffe Join at University of Delaware," *U.S. News & World Report*, October 19, 2009, www.usnews.com.
346. Joe Biden, *Promise Me, Dad*, 63; Schreckinger, *The Bidens*, 158.
347. Jill Biden, *Where the Light Enters*, 156; Osnos, *Joe Biden*, 99.
348. Biden Owens, *Growing Up Biden*, 270.
349. Levingston, *Barack and Joe*, 88.
350. News Journal, *Joe's Journey*, 97; Witcover, *Joe Biden*, 302.
351. News Journal, *Joe's Journey*, 108; Witcover, *Joe Biden*, 431.
352. Jill Biden, *Where the Light Enters*, 161.
353. News Journal, *Joe's Journey*, 23, 122, 125.
354. Witcover, *Joe Biden*, 442; Schreckinger, *The Bidens*, 180.
355. Levingston, *Barack and Joe*, 157; Witcover, *Joe Biden*, 436.
356. Biden Owens, *Growing Up Biden*, 171; Lienemann, *Biden*, 55.
357. Witcover, *Joe Biden*, 469.
358. Schreckinger, *The Bidens*, 165.
359. Lienemann, *Biden*, 102–3.
360. State of Delaware, "2010 General Election," November 5, 2010, www.elections.delaware.gov.
361. Rachel Kipp, "Matriarch Jean Was Source of Strength to Biden Family," *News Journal*, January 9, 2010, A1–A5.
362. Osnos, *Joe Biden*, 66–67.
363. Lienemann, *Biden*, 108; Federal Election Commission, "Federal Elections 2012," www.fec.gov; State of Delaware, "2012 General Election," November 14, 2012, elections.delaware.gov.

Chapter 17

364. Buhle, *If We Break*, 155; H. Biden, *Beautiful Things*, 13.
365. Joe Biden, *Promise Me, Dad*, 115; H. Biden, *Beautiful Things*, 17.
366. H. Biden, *Beautiful Things*, 10; Joe Biden, *Promise Me, Dad*, 33.
367. Joe Biden, *Promise Me, Dad*, 160.
368. Lienemann, *Biden*, 163.
369. Joe Biden, *Promise Me, Dad*, 161.
370. H. Biden, *Beautiful Things*, 9; Joe Biden, *Promise Me, Dad*, 139.
371. Jonathan Starkey, Cris Barrish and Xerxes Wilson, "Beau Biden Dies of Brain Cancer at 40," *News Journal*, May 31, 2015, A1–A17.
372. Maureen Milford and Jonathan Starkey, "Hand in Hand with His Humility Went Integrity, Friends Said," *News Journal*, June 1, 2015, A1–A5.

373. Joe Biden, *Beautiful Things*, 29.

374. Zebley, *Churches of Delaware*, 85–86.

375. W. Barksdale Maynard, "St. Anthony of Padua Church," SAH Archipedia, https://sah-archipedia.org/buildings/DE-01-WL77.

376. Zebley, *Churches of Delaware*, 86.

377. Schreckinger, *The Bidens*, 195.

378. H. Biden, *Beautiful Things*, 30.

379. Levingston, *Barack and Joe*, 246; Lienemann, *Biden*, 166.

380. Levingston, *Barack and Joe*, 249.

381. H. Biden, *Beautiful Things*, 110.

382. Joe Biden, *Promise Me, Dad*, 234–35.

383. 166th Airlift Wing, "National Guard Headquarters to be Named for Beau Biden," May 26, 2016, www.166aw.af.mil; Celia Cohen, "Major Beau," *Delaware Grapevine*, May 31, 2016, www.delawaregrapevine.com.

Chapter 18

384. Joe Biden, *Promise Me, Dad*, 199–200.

385. Jill Biden, *Where the Light Enters*, 193.

386. H. Biden, *Beautiful Things*, 213.

387. Witcover, *Joe Biden*, 305.

388. Joe Biden, *Promises to Keep*, 7.

389. Faggioli, *Biden and Catholicism*, 125.

390. Ibid., 133, 153–54.

391. Schreckinger, *The Bidens*, 98.

392. Faggioli, *Biden and Catholicism*, 5.

393. Cohen, *Only in Delaware*, 205.

394. Jill Biden, *Where the Light Enters*, 192.

395. "St. Joseph's Church, Brandywine Consecrated Yesterday," *Wilmington Daily Republican*, November 26, 1894, 1.

396. National Park Service, "St. Joseph's on the Brandywine," National Register of Historic Places registration form, July 13, 1976; Zebley, *Churches of Delaware*, 126–27; Saint Joseph on the Brandywine, "Parish History," www.stjosephonthebrandywine.org.

397. William P. Frank, "St. Joseph's-on-the-Brandywine Is Defying Cynics Who Predicted It Would Have to Close," *Journal-Every Evening*, December 6, 1941, 3.

398. Chris Flood, "President Joe Biden Enjoys Some Beach Time," *Cape Gazette*, July 11, 2023, www.capegazette.com; St. Edmond Roman Catholic Church, "Parish History," www.stedmond.org; "500 Attend

Dedication Rites at New Church in Rehoboth," *Morning News*, September 2, 1940, 3; "New Church for Rehoboth," *Journal-Every Evening*, May 19, 1940, 8.

399. Jill Biden, *Where the Light Enters*, 169; Osnos, *Joe Biden*, 111.

400. Jill Biden, *Where the Light Enters*, 179–80.

Chapter 19

401. Lienemann, *Biden*, 249.

402. Weitzman, *What's the Matter with Delaware?*, 64; Schreckinger, *The Bidens*, 204.

403. Josephine Peterson, "I-95 Welcome Center Renamed After Bidens," *News Journal*, September 17, 2018, www.delawareonline.com; Mark Eichmann, "Biden Name Will Welcome Millions of Travelers to Delaware," WHYY, September 18, 2018, www.whyy.org; EDiS Company, "The Biden Welcome Center," www.ediscompany.com.

404. Jill Biden, *Where the Light Enters*, 172; "Jill Biden Marks Keel-Laying of Submarine Delaware," Associated Press, April 30, 2016, www.delawareonline.com; Delaware Secretary of State, "Commissioning Commemoration," www.sos.delaware.gov.

405. Joe Biden, "We Are Living Through a Battle for the Soul of This Nation," *The Atlantic*, August 27, 2017, www.theatlantic.com.

406. Biden Owens, *Growing Up Biden*, 254; Osnos, *Joe Biden*, 6.

407. Osnos, *Joe Biden*, 138; Allen and Parnes, *Lucky*, 394.

408. Chase Center, "About the Chase Center," www.centerontheriverfront.com.

409. Mark Eichmann, "Wilmington's Queen Theatre Takes Center Stage in Biden Campaign," WHYY, October 25, 2020, www.whyy.org; Queen Wilmington, "About the Queen," www.thequeenwilmington.com; Delaware Public Media, "Live Nation's Takeover of the Queen Brings Changes," December 15, 2017, https://www.delawarepublic.org/culture-lifestyle-sports/2017-12-15/live-nations-takeover-of-the-queen-brings-changes.

410. Allen and Parnes, *Lucky*, 394, 404, 406.

Chapter 20

411. Ellen Driscoll, "Lewes Athlete Returns Lost Cufflink to Joe Biden," January 25, 2019, www.capegazette.com.

412. Ryan Mavity, "Biden Purchases Home in Rehoboth," *Cape Gazette*, June 8, 2017, www.capegazette.com; Will Weissert, "Joe Biden's Beach Hideaway Has Political Sun Shining on Delaware's Rehoboth Beach," Associated Press, November 15, 2020, www.usatoday.com; Chris Flood, "Two Presidential Candidates Have Homes in Rehoboth," *Cape Gazette*, May 24, 2019, www.capegazette.com.

413. Jeff Neiburg and Margie Fishman, "Rehoboth Beach Area Braces for the Biden Family," *Daily Times*, June 9, 2017, www.delmarvanow.com; Casey Tolan, "Biden's Delaware Vacation Home Faces 'Extreme' Flood Risk as Climate Change Leads to Rising Seas," CNN, September 13, 2022, www.cnn.com.

414. Chris Flood, "Wall around Biden's North Shores Home Is Finally Being Built," *Cape Gazette*, November 18, 2022, www.capegazette.com; Ron MacArthur, "Sussex BOA Approves Biden Fence Variances," *Cape Gazette*, April 5, 2022, www.capegazette.com.

415. Weissert, "Biden's Beach Hideaway"; Chris Flood, "When Biden's in Town, Rehoboth Working with Secret Service," *Cape Gazette*, December 18, 2020, www.capegazette.com; Darlene Superville, "Biden Says He Went to His House in Rehoboth Beach, Delaware, Because He Can't Go 'Home Home,'" Associated Press, September 3, 2023, www.apnews.com.

416. Chris Flood, "President Biden Expected to Be in Town Oct. 20," *Cape Gazette*, October 18, 2023, www.capegazette.com; Bill Shull, "Bidens Take Extended Vacation in Rehoboth," *Cape Gazette*, August 4, 2023, www.capegazette.com.

417. Chris Flood, "Biden Signs Welcome Poster Made by Henlopen Acres Family," *Cape Gazette*, December 29, 2021, www.capegazette.com

418. Chris Flood, "Bidens at Breakfast at Egg in Rehoboth Beach," *Cape Gazette*, October 23, 2023, www.capegazette.com; Weissert, "Biden's Beach Hideaway."

419. Barbara Sprunt, "What a Beach Vacation Looks Like for President Biden," NPR, August 3, 2023, www.npr.org; Neiburg and Fishman, "Rehoboth Beach."

420. Dennis Forney, "Major Projects in Works at Cape Henlopen State Park," *Cape Gazette*, September 17, 2021, www.capegazette.com; Molly Murray, "Henlopen Park Gets More Land," *News Journal*, October 9, 1996, 1–2; Ron MacArthur, "Cape Henlopen State Park Celebrates 50 Years," *Cape Gazette*, September 26, 2014, www.capegazette.com.

421. Chris Flood, "Before Bike Bobble, Biden Takes Herring Point Selfie," *Cape Gazette*, June 20, 2022, www.capegazette.com.

422. Scott Cameron, "Jill Biden Signs Books at Browseabout in Rehoboth," *Cape Gazette*, July 3, 2019, www.capegazette.com; Weissert, "Biden's Beach Hideaway."

423. Neiburg and Fishman, "Rehoboth Beach."

Chapter 21

424. "30 Things Joe Biden Did as President You Might Have Missed," *Politico Magazine*, February 2, 2024, www.politico.com.

SELECTED BIBLIOGRAPHY

Allen, Jonathan, and Amie Parnes. *Lucky: How Joe Biden Barely Won the Presidency.* New York: Crown, 2021.

Biden, Hunter. *Beautiful Things: A Memoir.* New York: Gallery Books, 2021.

Biden, Jill. *Where the Light Enters: Building a Family, Discovering Myself.* New York: Flatiron Books, 2019.

Biden, Joe. *Promise Me, Dad: A Year of Hope, Hardship, and Purpose.* New York: Flatiron Books, 2017.

———. *Promises to Keep.* New York: Random House, 2007.

Biden Owens, Valerie. *Growing Up Biden: A Memoir.* New York: Celadon Books, 2022.

Buhle, Kathleen. *If We Break: A Memoir of Marriage, Addiction, and Healing.* New York: Crown, 2022.

Cohen, Celia. *Only in Delaware: Politics and Politicians in the First State.* Newark, DE: Grapevine Publishing, 2002.

Cramer, Richard Ben. *What It Takes: The Way to the White House.* New York: Vintage Books, 1993.

Faggioli, Massimo. *Joe Biden and Catholicism in the United States.* New London, CT: Bayard, 2021.

Frank, Bill. *Bill Frank's Delaware: Six Decades through the Eyes of a Working Newspaperman.* Wilmington, DE: Middle Atlantic Press, 1987.

Levingston, Steven. *Barack and Joe: The Making of an Extraordinary Partnership.* New York: Hachette Books, 2019.

Lienemann, David. *Biden: The Obama Years and the Battle for the Soul of America.* New York: Hachette, 2020.

News Journal. *Joe's Journey: Biden's Rise to Vice President.* New Castle, DE: Quebecor World Inc., 2009.

Osnos, Evan. *Joe Biden: The Life, the Run, and What Matters Now.* New York: Scribner, 2020.

Schreckinger, Ben. *The Bidens: Inside the First Family's Fifty-Year Rise to Power.* New York: Twelve, 2021.

Weitzman, Hal. *What's the Matter with Delaware? How the First State Has Favored the Rich, Powerful, and Criminal—And How It Costs Us All.* Princeton, NJ: Princeton University Press, 2022.

Whipple, Chris. *The Fight of His Life: Inside Joe Biden's White House.* New York: Scribner, 2023.

Witcover, Jules. *Joe Biden: A Life of Trial and Redemption.* New York: William Morrow and Co., 2010.

Zebley, Frank. *The Churches of Delaware.* Wilmington: Frank Zebley, 1947.

INDEX

ABOUT THE AUTHOR

Dan Shortridge is an author and historian based in Philadelphia who has a passion for uncovering obscure stories from local history.

He began his career in journalism as a reporter, copy editor and news editor with the *Chronicle-Telegram* in Elyria, Ohio; the *Daily Times* of Salisbury, Maryland.; and the *News Journal* of Wilmington, Delaware. He has led communications and marketing in Delaware for the Delaware Department of Agriculture, the Delaware State Housing Authority and the Sussex Technical School District. He works on content creation, research and editing for a mid-Atlantic marketing firm serving nonprofit organizations.

He also does résumé writing and career consulting, has written a careers column for several Ohio newspapers, runs a regional marketing and communications jobs list and speaks frequently on communications, marketing and career topics.

Dan's writing has appeared in the *Baltimore Sun, Campaigns & Elections, Camping, Scouting, CampBusiness, School Administrator* and *Construction Business Owner.*

His books include *DIY Public Relations: Telling Your Story on a Zero-Dollar Budget; Lost Delaware; Secret Delaware;* and *100 Things to Do in Delaware Before You Die,* all three written with Rachel Kipp; and *Go Forth to Serve: A History of Henson Scout Reservation,* written with the late Ken Gerlach.

Dan has won multiple honors for his work, including a Sigma Delta Chi team award from the Society of Professional Journalists; an Ochberg fellowship from the Dart Center for Journalism and Trauma; and multiple book awards from the Delaware Press Association.

He enjoys discovering new bookstores, exploring the outdoors and writing footnotes.

Visit us at
www.historypress.com